Critical and Historical Principles
of Literary History

Critical and Historical Principles of Literary History

R. S. Crane

With a Foreword by Sheldon Sacks

The University of Chicago Press
Chicago and London

First published as a chapter in *The Idea of the Humanities
and Other Essays, Critical and Historical*, by R. S. Crane
(2 vols., University of Chicago Press, 1967)

The University of Chicago Press, Chicago 60637
The University of Chicago Press, Ltd., London

© 1967, 1971 by The University of Chicago. All rights reserved
Published 1971
Printed in the United States of America

Library of Congress Catalog Card Number: 75–159832
International Standard Book Number: 0–226–11826–6

Foreword

Sheldon Sacks

1

Typical of his most penetrating essays, "Critical and Historical Principles of Literary History" was intended, as R. S. Crane himself tells us, "as a means of clarifying my own ideas on the subject." This aim seems sufficiently modest, but Crane's standard of what constituted clarification, abrasively rigorous when applied to the efforts of other critics, was impossibly demanding when he measured the value of his own work. He was never satisfied that he had achieved his goal.

That a hiatus of seventeen years separated Crane's attempt at "clarification" and its publication shortly before his death was more frustrating than surprising to students, friends, and colleagues who had in the past only rarely succeeded in persuading or, more accurately, cajoling him into publishing crucial essays that he believed too tentative for general dissemination. In fact, some had resorted on occasion to "pirating" lectures and manuscripts for mimeographed distribution to an increasing—though hardly a universal—group of admirers who, on the whole a contentious bunch influenced by Crane himself to accept nothing on the basis of authority alone, discovered even in their disagreements with him that special source of intellectual excitement that arises only when we witness the encounter of a brilliant mind grappling with problems too significant and thorny for facile or definitive solutions.

Indeed, as students encountering Crane's work for the first time will quickly discover, that fine sense of excitement—the special pleasure consequent on our successfully meeting a challenge to expand our very capacity for understanding—is not accessible to the casual reader of Crane's criticism. Instead, the student is asked to become a full participant in a difficult exploration led by a guide who makes no allowances for intellectual flabbiness or lapses of concentration. Assuming that his reader, like himself, is fully committed to the importance of a joint enterprise, he makes no effort to coax him into climbing one more peak for the sake of discovering another crag, previously unseen, but waiting on the horizon. It is only for the serious student of literature or, as we shall see, of history, that Crane's work has immense value. By "serious" student I mean to imply not only one who has been deeply moved by literary works, or even one convinced of the importance to civilization itself of artistic creation, but one who, in addition to sharing that experience and conviction, possess so strong a degree of intellectual curiosity that he will actively seek the best possible answers—no matter how difficult—to the most fruitful questions—no matter how complex—about the nature, genesis, and value of those "monuments of [the soul's] magnificence." Crane may at times make great demands on both the literary sensibilities and intellectual resources even of such students, but he will never patronize them by denying the validity of their literary experience or betray them by reducing the complexities of human creativity to simplistic formulas or neat dichotomies.

For example, though intensely interested in problems of critical methodology, he shuns the very idea of creating some method which, mechanically applied, will result in automatic interpretations of new literary works; such a notion of methology is, for Crane, the clearest sign of mere dogma, the greatest enemy of serious inquiry. Again, though much of his professional life was devoted to a search for formal principles on which particular literary works have been and can be constructed, he stigmatizes as one of the "characteristic corruptions" of structural analysis "the disposition to reduce problems of artistic form to questions of 'structure' merely, in abstraction from the humanly interesting and moving aspects of works upon which their form in the full sense of its peculiar moral and emotional quality depends." Or, widely known (and often condemned) as a "generic critic," he argues that critical corruption occurs "most disastrously from the natural tendency to force individual works into formal molds that are . . . inappropriate to them."

Yet it *is* true that Crane is both a "generic" and a "formal" critic, and one cannot begin to understand the exciting potentialities of the "narrative history of forms" he describes and proposes in the following essay without some grasp of the complex relationship he postulates between the "humanly interesting and moving aspects" of literature and the creation, in unique works, of new literary effects, techniques, and even forms by writers as they discover new potentialities latent in general principles on which varieties of literary works are constructed. To put this in another way, in his best criticism Crane succeeds in showing us not only how a given work is unique but how it is unique as a literary construct, "a concrete whole" that embodies—or, more accurately—formalizes "humanly interesting and moving" action, character, thought, feeling, made significant as artistic creation.

In a few illustrative remarks in *The Languages of Criticism and the Structure of Poetry,* for example, he asks us to see *Macbeth* as a literary event of even greater significance than the creation of one more masterpiece of Shakespearean drama. He reveals how each part of the play contributes to the moving force of an action whose protagonist plausibly commits such monstrous deeds that his destruction grows increasingly desirable, indeed necessary, for the sake of the suffering world around him; to this extent the "structure" of the play would be analogous to that of such "punitive actions" as *The Duchess of Malfi* or *The Jew of Malta,* dramas whose overall effects depend, unlike those of classical tragedy, upon the satisfaction we feel at the punishment of dangerous and destructive villains. Yet, aware that the peculiar emotional force of *Macbeth* cannot be explained as the consequence of even the most perfect representation of an action constructed on the principles of "punitive drama," Crane perceives and makes us perceive how Shakespeare uses every technical, structural, and linguistic device at his masterly command to reveal the increasing intensity of Macbeth's own terrible suffering as a consequence of qualities so human—even humane—that we are made simultaneously to desire his death as much for his own sake as for that of the world made victim to his monstrosity. The emotional richness and complexity of the whole play—conceived of as "an artistic synthesis"—can be seen then as the consequence of the "humanly interesting and moving aspects" of a unique literary experience made possible by Shakespeare's brilliant and profound creation of a new *form* of tragic plot which is, nevertheless, [a special realization of general principles] on which good, bad, or indifferent tragedies are constructed. *Macbeth*, in other words, represents a crucial new development of tragedy and, therefore, of literature.

But to say this about *Macbeth* is meaningless if there are no general principles of tragedy, and it is empty if we cannot begin to investigate and specify them. We might then just well say that *Macbeth* is a crucial new development of cookbooks, or of sermons, or of disinterested philosophical inquiries. And if this is true, there can be neither development nor change in literature, but only specifiable differences among works that we arbitrarily classify as literary.

On the other hand, if we mistake conventional "rules" current at any one period for literary principles; if we fail to consider the great variety of artistic ends that have been and may be pursued by good poets; or if—to sum it up—we falsify or simplify our characterization of structural principles by any of a host of corruptions that threaten us as critics, then, to that extent, we will be unable to specify the distinctive powers of *Macbeth*, conceived of as a "concrete literary whole," and our history will prove as inaccurate as our criticism was inept. For the literary historian who attempts what Crane calls "a narrative history of forms," the unique literary work conceived of as "a concrete whole" *becomes* the event with which he deals, and his task

> is not to clarify literary particulars by treating them as "parts" of more easily apprehended wholes. Rather it is to preserve the integrity of particular literary achievements while making them intelligible historically in terms (*a*) of the individual acts that resulted in their production and (*b*) of the context of continuous changes in literary forms, materials, and techniques to which these acts were related as effects or causes. . . . The only ultimate realities he will be concerned with are literary works conceived of as concrete wholes possessing distinctive powers by virtue of the peculiar manner in which their diverse elements were selected, treated, and combined. He must attempt both to trace the separable elements to their origins and to account for their treatment and combination, and this with reference always to observable differences in the principles of construction upon which the final result depended in different works.

This, of course, is not that facile concept of "literary history" derived from a college outline series or from those survey courses that consist of a potpourri of generalizations about social and political milieux which, mixed generously with assorted biographical information, purport in some way, always undefined, to "explain" large numbers of literary works skimmed by students in chronological order.

On the contrary, to attempt even a fragment of a "narrative history of forms" is a difficult pursuit that demands the highest use of our literary sensibilities and challenges us to expose the intellectual poverty of our critical conceptions in order that, in the end, we may enrich and refine them. For the serious student of literature, to pursue such a history as Crane describes is to engage in an activity absolutely central to increasing conceptually our understanding of literary works *as* literary works with the reward of fuller and richer revelation of the changing artistry, value, and genesis of those monuments of human creativity that initially moved us and captured our imaginations. For the serious student of history, Crane's essay must raise questions as crucial and central as, let us say, those raised by Collingwood or Popper about the very nature of what constitutes historical "events," or historical "facts" and how these may be related to each other in causal histories that result in an adequate and revealing account of change and development.

To realize the promise latent in Crane's proposal for a "narrative history of forms" the historian must understand the problems and master the conventional disciplines of literary criticism, and the literary critic must understand the kinds of questions traditionally raised by historians and what kinds of criteria are appropriate to measure the adequacy of the answers to such questions. But that is precisely what is so revolutionary about all of R. S. Crane's work: his conservative insistence that, whatever our specialty, no matter how different our points of departure and the routes we must travel, the philosopher, the linguist, the historian, the critic will arrive somewhere in range of his destination only to the degree that he has become an accomplished humanist en route.

2

Writing in 1971 it seems almost quaint to recall that there was a time in the early and middle thirties when literary criticism was not considered a respectable pursuit for students of literature in American universities, and that it required an intellectual revolution before it won a place in the academic curriculum "at least coordinate with linguistics, philology, literary history, and the history of ideas." One of the earliest and most powerful voices raised in favor of change was R. S. Crane's, especially persuasive because of his own reputation as a historical scholar. In 1935 he argued that "literary history . . . has occupied too privileged a place, especially during recent years. . . . Research has been our watchword, and with results we need not be ashamed of; but for the most part we have narrowed the meaning of the term until it has come to stand, not broadly for responsible and original inquiries of all sorts but specifically for inquiries among documents pursued for strictly historical ends. Our teaching meantime has taken a similar course." The consequence of such narrowed pursuit and teaching, "our unforgivable fault," was that "in comparison with students of the better sort trained in the schools and universities of England and France, our students, even our most capable ones, tend to be esthetic barbarians."

If such comments were unlikely to increase Crane's popularity with the "establishment" of the thirties, his assessment in 1957 of the results of the accomplished "revolution" seem almost designed to antagonize the now victorious and increasingly ubiquitous critical schools. In "Criticism as Inquiry; or, The Perils of the 'High Priori Road' " he proclaimed emphatically that he had been "embarrassed by René Wellek's and Austin Warren's commendation of the Department of English at Chicago for having 'boldly reoriented' its whole graduate program 'from the historical to the critical.' The 'critical' is there, assuredly, but so also is the 'historical,' and in such a relation to the 'critical,' in intention at least, that neither can be separated from the other." He is willing to state quite baldly, "There can be no adequate criticism that is not based on the history of the art with which it is concerned." What Crane in 1935 had "failed to predict was that the immediate future at least belonged to those radical reformers of literary study—soon to be called, loosely, 'new critics'—who were in revolt not merely against the limitations of the older learning but, as it has turned out, against the very conception of intellectual method that gave it its status as a learning."

Where Crane had battled for the intellectual status of criticism as a crucial form of inquiry and for the consequent education of students and teachers "capable of intelligently discussing an imaginative work in terms appropriate to its nature," the victory had gone to the criticism of the "ruling hypothesis" and the "dialectical fallacy," less revealing and more anti-intellectual than the limited historicism it had replaced:

> Behind each of the hypotheses [of popular academic critics] I have cited is a fashionable critical belief, about the validity or general applicability of which the writer raises no questions—the belief that multiple meaning is an essential property of poetry; the belief that the unifying significance of a poetic drama is normally given by its patterns of recurrent imagery; the belief that literary structure is typically a matter of "ironical tension"; the belief that the dominant problem of most novelists—of Jane Austen, for example—is one of sexual adjustment; the belief that serious works of fiction are likely to embody concealed allegories. And it is these general premises of theory rather than particular premises drawn from history or the text or our natural responses to it, that actually do most of the work of demonstration. You only have to consider how little would be left in any of these studies, beyond mere conjecture and particular observation, were the critic suddenly to lose faith in the general postulates he has adopted!

In fact, there would be little difference between the procedures of fashionable criticism and those of "theologians who set out to demonstrate the workings of divine providence in the facts of history or of the physical world," if we were to substitute for "divine providence" such terms as "symbolism," "plurisignation," or "archetypal universality."

"Critical and Historical Principles of Literary History" was written seven years before these quoted remarks, and it is clear that Crane's justifiable fears that current literary criticism represented a dangerous threat to intellectual method, to serious inquiry, and to the intellectual content of humanistic study itself were largely responsible for his attempt at positive clarification of his views. Furthermore, his fear of the ease with which the half-truths of current dogma had become apotheosized as universal critical principles was partly responsible, I believe, for his describing as an "uncompleted short monograph" an inquiry that succeeds, as completely as any single essay could, not only in delineating the "principles both critical and historical which have most commonly governed the writing of literary history since the origins of that discipline," but in providing us with an adequate account of "another mode of interpreting historical differences in literature of which we have had thus far only sporadic and fragmentary examples"—the narrative history of forms that characterizes the concrete wholes created by poets and treats them as the events to be related to each other in ways that reveal significant literary change or development.

As he investigates what has been done and compares past accomplishments with future possibilities, without in any way reducing his pluralistic concern for the enormous variety of legitimate kinds of questions applicable to artistic creation, Crane inevitably probes for and reveals basic principles that underlie any serious study of literature when that study is conceived of as a discipline, or, as he liked to call it, a "learning." The terms "definitive" or even "exhaustive" must always remain in some sense inapplicable to such inquiries, since their very virtues are measured as much by the fruitfulness of the new questions they raise as by the adequacy and permanence of the tentative answers they provide. Consequently, some feeling of incompleteness must always trouble the explorer who rejects the plausible philosophical triviality or, to use Crane's favorite metaphor, who leaves "the high priori road" to knowledge and instead attempts "to develop gradually a body of general knowledge of literature—a little now, more perhaps tomorrow—that is grounded in literary history and practical experience of writing, instead of in dialectic merely; and by inculcating, finally, in our teaching and practice an exploratory and inquiring rather than a doctrinaire use of such knowledge in studies of particular works and writers." And, indeed, Crane strove mightily throughout his professional lifetime to cultivate that "exploratory and inquiring spirit" at least as much in his teaching as in his own writing. "Responsible and original inquiries of all sorts" were pursued with the same rigor and enthusiasm in his classrooms as in his essays or books.

In 1956, in "a penitentiary spirit," he writes a revealing account of his own goals as a teacher. He recounts:

> It may have been because I had just been reading examinations or term papers; but in any event I had begun to reflect, in no self-flattering mood, on how little I had done, on the whole, to enable my students to stand on their own feet after they left me—every man equipped to be, in a sensible way, his own critic. I thought of those students who had done good work for me, and on whom I believed I had made an impression at the time;

and I couldn't help wondering, pessimistically, how many of them, after five or a dozen years, were still able, on their own, to think as well, critically, about a new modern book or an old one they were reading for the first time as they had been able to think about the texts they had discussed under the immediate pressure of my assignments. . . . I *should* have had many more students of all sorts, it seemed to me, about whom I could feel sure that, in their later dealings with literature, they had become something more than users or victims of the criticism of others, including that which I myself had exposed them to.

He proceeds to contrast two teachers of history to whom he had been exposed as a student. Professor A had been "a brilliant and fluent lecturer" for whom "the problem of teaching history was simply the problem of communicating effectively a concrete and self-contained subject matter; of putting before us a particular body of facts and generalizations which had presumably been thought about critically and independently by himself and others but which he didn't think about in our presence and which it was our duty—our whole duty—merely to assimilate and remember as long as we could. . . . I cannot recall any question in history, in any field, that I have since been able to think about more intelligently, or with any surer grasp of what an answer to it might involve, by virtue of Professor A's teaching."

Professor B, on the other hand, "taught as a guide rather than as a master, as an inquiring student of history like ourselves, only more advanced"; though he, too, lectured, he did so "in a problematic rather than a didactic spirit; making explicit to us, as he went along, exactly what he was doing and why, taking us inside the processes of reasoning he brought to bear on his problems." And, perhaps most important of all, though he did build "superstructures of historical interpretation, . . . these were never detached . . . from the foundations in primary concepts of human problems, reasons, and actions upon which they were erected. And the longer I have attempted to teach literature to students at all levels, from freshmen to advanced graduates, the more convinced I have become of the wisdom of his procedure." This is not to imply that Professor B was less exacting about historical facts than A; for B also,

history could not be taught except through the teaching of particular historical subjects that were assumed to be worth knowing as thoroughly as we could know them for their own sake. Such knowledge was an end which he kept firmly in view in all his courses, but it was not, as for Professor A, the final end of what he tried to do for us. He knew that most of it was bound to pass away sooner or later, after we had ceased to study with him; and I don't believe that this greatly worried him. He was, for one thing, too wise a historian not to be aware of the probable impermanence, for himself and other scholars, as well as for us, of any particular historical interpretations he might offer. But more than this, he was quite consciously concerned with implanting in us . . . something over and above his immediate subject matter that might possibly remain with us for the rest of our lives, whether we became historians in a professional sense or not. This something was the discipline of history, which he thought of as a special but universally applicable way of considering human beings and their individual and collective actions, and of getting warranted knowledge concerning them. Whatever we did in later life, he thought, we ought all to be historians in this broader sense of having as a permanent possession the habit of good historical thinking. . . . He was pleased when we answered well . . . subject-matter questions . . . but he was far more pleased when we gave some slight evidence . . . that we were perhaps beginning to learn how to ask good historical questions on our own and to deal with them independently of anything he had told us. That was a sign—and the sign he always took most seriously—that we were actually profiting from his teaching.

If such a view of education in the humanities were generally adopted, if all of us who are teachers (as well as learners) sought for such a sign as the minimum verification that we were inquiring and helping others to inquire in that broad and humane sense described by Crane, the implications for education, especially in departments of English, might be profound. When such a sign becomes the desideratum of all our teaching and learning—for Crane merely dual aspects of the same process of inquiry—our efforts as students or teachers can never terminate merely in discovering or conveying such facts as are accessible to the "researcher," though research is a necessary ingredient in all serious inquiry, and inquiry itself can reveal nothing without the firmest grasp of the facts it purports to explain. Such a squabble as one now current about whether the Ph.D. should become a "teaching" rather than a "research degree" (at best a misnomer, at worst a distortion of educational goals) would prove meaningless at any university where teaching itself was viewed as joint intellectual inquiry. Artificial antitheses such as those between general and specialized, graduate and undergraduate, liberal and professional educations, would generate far less heat, and we could see them then as "useful only in helping us to think about our ends in education—the good of as many as possible of our students." For, in fact, the means to a general education in the sense that Crane describes it in "Every Man His Own Critic" may be as specialized or technical as we please.

I can make no attempt here fully to outline Crane's views on education and, certainly, I am not trying to suggest that any conceivable transformation of English departments or even whole universities will result in social concord, a richer life for the many, or even—if that were desirable—an end to "student unrest." The furthest extent of my ambition has been to draw the reader's attention, during another "revolutionary" period of education in the humanities, to the implications of Crane's work for the teaching and study of literature in this "rhetorical aside"—rhetorical because I have been writing, obviously, as an advocate whose own professional life has been significantly shaped by Crane's views; an aside because it concentrates on what "Critical and Historical Principles of Literary Criticism" implies rather than attempting further clarification of Crane's explicit formulations, at best a supererogatory endeavor that could result only in oversimplification of his treatise.

The time does seem out of joint, however, to attempt to gain wider currency for Crane's views about the importance of the study of literature as a discipline, a "learning," for his interpretation of teaching as humane but rigorous intellectual inquiry "never detached from the foundations in primary concepts of human problems, reasons, and actions" that give significance to our attempts to explain the moving force of literary works. Phrases like "rational discourse" and "serious inquiry," never especially congenial to many students of literature content to interpret exercises in sensibility as intellectual pursuit, have descended to that nadir of usage that allows them to function as the self-ridiculing stock in trade of any tyro academic satirist. The idea that the "life of the mind," the enlargement of conceptual understanding, is a goal worth pursuing for its own sake has, for a variety of reasons, including academe's failure to pursue it, been reduced to something less than an academic joke: its profession is seen as a sure sign of hypocrisy and social indifference not only by the young but by many who, like myself, scraping middle age, feel pressed to renew credentials as men of social conscience by heralding educational revolution that stresses relevance at the expense of intellectual significance (even though this will surely result in the bankruptcy of both virtues).

It is widely assumed that a purely intellectual approach to education has been tried, its sterility exposed, its abandonment in favor of some undefined but more meaningful learning experience seen as a burning necessity. Ironically, absolute commitment to intellectual pursuit has rarely if ever been attempted in American universities, and we should hardly be surprised when students sensitive to the moral and social horrors of our time demand that we transform our institutions into what, alas, will inevitably be third-rate centers of social service and social reform. The argument that such a transformation will destroy the university's capacity to perform the only crucial service for society that it and it alone is equipped to perform well must ring hollow to the extent that universities themselves have failed to embody intellectual goals as the object of a joint pursuit by students and faculty. Unfortunately, departments of English, our largest collection of humanists now, have been traditionally though perhaps unconsciously the most anti-intellectual. It is no accident that the intellectual revolution Crane heralded in 1935 was leveled against the narrow historicism that arbitrarily barred "responsible and original inquiries of all sorts," or that, in 1957, he had to interpret the replacement of serious inquiry by critical dogma as an attack on intellectual method itself. But it will indeed be "our unforgivable fault" if, during this time of passionate attack on the very notion that truth matters or even exists, we join or even passively accept a new revolution that consciously promises to make anti-intellectuality a primary virtue of humanistic education.

Needless to say we must continue to convey our own enthusiasm for literature by any means at our disposal since, if students are not moved by their experience with literary works, there is nothing worth their inquiring into. Yet, though it is not obvious and though it is difficult to achieve, we have been shown with a kind of lovely clarity by at least one great teacher and inquirer how intellectual inquiry can and should play the crucial central role in a literary education that becomes more humane and significant by virtue of its intellectual rigor.

I am tempted to make other sweeping statements in this rhetorical aside but, as I write, I cannot help recalling my final argument with R. S. Crane, who, in the hospital a few weeks before his death, punctured for the last time one of my pretentious generalizations as much by the characteristic twinkle in "those ancient glittering eyes" as by his politely growled, "Sacks, where is your evidence for that statement?" If only he had asked the question about my remarks in this introduction, I could at least have suggested to him that he read with his usual care and understanding "Critical and Historical Principles of Literary History," one of the most profound humanistic inquiries of our time.

*Critical and Historical Principles
of Literary History*

M Y INTENTION in this essay is to inquire into the principles, both critical and historical, which have most commonly governed the writing of literary history since the origins of that discipline in ancient Greece, and to contrast with these the principles of another mode of interpreting historical differences in literature of which we have had thus far only sporadic and fragmentary examples. And the first question to be considered is naturally that of the materials out of which all varieties of literary history construct their propositions.

1. CRITICAL ELEMENTS

The propositions of any history of literature that is not confined to the external conditions of literary activity necessarily comprise elements of two kinds: terms signifying actions, characters, habits, aims, and circumstances of writers, and terms signifying attributes of literary works; without the latter the history would not be a history of literature and without the former it would not be a history. The elements of the first sort are derived by the techniques of historical research from an examination of available documents, in the light of general knowledge concerning human behavior; their character in any history is relative to the state of the materials and to the histori-

1

an's intelligence, training, and industry. The elements of the second sort are derived by critical analysis from literary texts, in the light of theoretical assumptions concerning the nature of literary works and the kinds of significant statements that can be made about them; their character in any history is relative to the historian's literary sensitivity but even more decisively to the particular scheme of critical and historical principles which he brings to his task.

It is possible therefore to have as many different schools of literary history as there are schools of literary criticism—or, as we shall see later, schools of historical interpretation. For our purposes only the most far-reaching differences in critical theory need be considered, and we may begin by observing that most literary histories, however great their diversity in other respects, have presupposed a conception of imaginative literature (or poetry) which does not differentiate essentially, but only accidentally, between one of its species and others, or between any of these and writing in general. Differentiations of many kinds, determined by varied criteria, have of course been made, but their warrant has not been found in the principles of construction peculiar to different literary arts but rather in the possibilities of variation inherent generally in human discourse viewed as the joint product of reason and speech. The clearest sign of this is that we have had few literary histories in which the analysis of works, irrespective of kind, does not turn on one simple and ancient distinction—the only one, in fact, basic to a consideration of discourse as such. This has been stated variously as a distinction between things and words, content and form, matter and manner, thought and expression, intention and language, or meaning and symbol. (In addition, arrangement often appears as a third term, necessitated by the fact that, as Quintilian remarked, "not only what we say and how we say it is of importance, but also the circumstances under which we say it.")

There have been many different ways, in this tradition, of viewing the nature of poetic or imaginative discourse—sometimes as expression, sometimes as communication, sometimes as statement, sometimes as resolution of practical problems, and so on—and, correspondingly, many different shifts in the constitution of the two fundamental elements, content and words, and of the relationship between them. From the Hellenistic grammarians and Roman rhetoricians to the "new critics" of the present day, however, some kind of

2

reduction of the various particular forms of poetry, drama, and fiction to modes of discourse has been well-nigh omnipresent in both criticism and literary history; and so seldom has the assumption on which it rests been challenged that some effort is now needed to realize that this assumption is after all not grounded in the nature of things. The reduction itself may or may not be an error in method, but once made it necessarily restricts the historian to such statements about the individual and collective differences exhibited by literary works as can be derived by the permutation and combination, the separation and conjunction, of attributes which any form of poetry may have in common with any other mode of discourse.

There are two ways in which such attributes may be discovered and employed in the characterization and differentiation of works. The first is the way of the philologist or, to give him his ancient name, the grammarian; it consists in the literal exegesis and comparison of texts in terms of the material traits of their content and form in a context of the circumstances of their composition; its essential instruments are textual and historical criticism, grammar (including prosody), the grammatical parts of logic, and bibliography in the traditional sense. With this equipment, and with a common-sense knowledge of human affairs, it is possible to make many precise and verifiable statements about literary texts such as any literary historian, whatever else he may be interested in doing, can neglect only at his scholarly peril. By means of a controlled grammatical reading of any text, its ostensible meanings and intentions can be revealed, its argument disengaged, its language described in linguistic or prosodic terms, and its structure, at least in the more obvious topical aspects of this, made manifest; by means of a comparison of different texts, works can be assigned to their respective genres (either those already defined and named by earlier poets and grammarians or others now first isolated and baptized). Themes, doctrines, images, styles, and other features of content or form can also be identified in terms of the earlier or contemporary traditions they reflect, as when historians point to the conventions of courtly love in Chaucer's *Troilus,* the Franciscan doctrines in Rabelais, the mixture of Newtonian and Shaftesburian ideas in Thomson's *Seasons,* the Dickensian characters in the early Henry James, or the Miltonic traits of verse and imagery in Collins and Gray. The state-

3

ments thus generated represent knowledge, never of the character of a work as an artistic whole, however, but only of the character of its substantive or "formal" parts; moreover, these are defined in terms of accidents of composition and of the historical affinities of the work with other works having parts that show similar material traits, never in terms of the artistic use of such parts. Most histories depending upon this mode of analysis compare and contrast parts of one work with those of another in terms of differences of kind; but the different kinds tend to be little more than convenient classes derived from obvious differences in the motives and interests of writers, or mere descriptive formulas for the traditions of subject matter or technique which a particular writer or group of writers happened to follow. All the familiar genres are thus reduced to conventions historically determined—tragedy and comedy no less than pastoral, ode, epistle, or sonnet—their distinctions resting upon differences not of constructive principle but merely of opinion and taste, such as are amenable to philological discussion without recourse to any analysis of forms.

The second way of defining the characters and differences of works depends similarly upon the assumption that all kinds of discourse, whether practical or artistic, didactic or mimetic, serious or comic, narrative, dramatic, or lyric, can be discussed significantly in terms of a single set of elements and principles. Unlike the first mode, however, its primary reference is not to the historical origins of works but to their effects upon readers. Its major concern, therefore, is not to describe the material and conventional traits of dramas, novels, and poems, although it may subsume these in its characterizations. Its concern is to discriminate their qualities or "values," not the qualities or values, be it noted, which *Macbeth,* for example, possesses because it is a particular kind of tragedy constructed according to particular principles, which were not all equally operative in the construction of *Othello,* but the qualities or values which any work shares with any other work by partaking in the common causes of all human discourse—language, the mind, society, history, and so on.

Now any element that may enter into a literary work—verse, diction, technique, structure, subject matter, attitude, doctrine, and the like—or any distinguishable complex of these, may have predicates of quality attached to it. And the number of such predicates that may be applied to any work is infinite, since, in the absence of principles differentiating species of work, there is no way, merely by looking at particular poems or dramas, of distinguishing between their essential and their accidental traits. This is why criticism in the qualitative mode has often seemed arbitrary and chaotic to outsiders who have compared the judgments of different critics on the same work. This need not be true for any given critic or school of critics, but if criticism of this sort is to be guaranteed against mere whimsy or irrelevance, the critic must be a philosopher. At least he must be a philosopher to the extent of possessing a general dialectical schematism appropriate to the discussion of any kind of discourse. This alone will enable him to give definition and compendency to his qualitative terms and will guide him in applying them to writers and works. An indefinite number of such schematisms is possible in criticism and literary history, since the structure of terms in any one of them is determined not by inductive investigation into the natures of works as particular kinds of concrete objects but by a logically prior analogizing of poetry to something else. The analogy may be negative, as when poetry is taken as a property of language and is then defined by contrasting it with the language of science or of practical life, or it may be positive, as when poetry is equated with psychological or moral activity, or with the making of myths and symbols, or with scientific or historical inquiry (as in contemporary discussions of prose fiction as "exploration"), and so on. The variety of available analogues for poetry (as for anything else) is without predictable limit, and thus there will always be a "new criticism" with every new generation if not with every new critic. Once the analogue is determined, however, the common necessities of the dialectical method begin to operate. The essence of the procedure, as Plato pointed out, is composition and division—division for the sake of achieving discriminations among particulars and composition for the sake of defining their unity. The consequence, in any writing regulated by the method, is a proliferation of predicate terms paired as contraries or opposites, which in their application to any subject are either separated or joined (sometimes by mere addition, sometimes by the mediation of a third term) to yield propositions and proofs.

In the long period from Greek antiquity to the present nearly all the practical criticism of professed critics (at least outside the techni-

5

cal tradition of Aristotle) and most literary histories concerned with values have been dominated by this preoccupation with the universally predicable qualities of literature as selected and ordered by some scheme of dialectical oppositions and resolutions. The discriminating contraries have been borrowed from many types of discourse—ethical, political, sociological, historical, mechanical, physiological, psychological, psychoanalytical, medical, metaphysical, epistemological, logical, grammatical, rhetorical, semantic—and the unifying devices have ranged from the ethical notion of value as a mean between extremes, characteristic of most criticism through the eighteenth century, to the psychological concept of value as a synthesis of opposite or discordant qualities characteristic of the neo-Coleridgean criticism of our time. There has been much diversity also in other respects: as between those critics and historians who have been clearly aware of the philosophic premises of their schemes (for example, Coleridge and Croce) and those, the great majority, who have not; as between those who, though not philosophers themselves, have conceived of practical criticism as a kind of knowledge (for example, Johnson) and those who have reduced it to a simple rhetoric of praise and blame pursued frequently in a routine spirit (for example, many otherwise distinguished scholars who venture on judgments of quality in their histories); finally, as between those who operate with a comprehensive scheme of qualities deduced from a complex analogue (for example, Johnson and Coleridge) and those who make all their discriminations in terms of one or two very general contrarieties (for example, I. A. Richards, F. R. Leavis, William Empson, Cleanth Brooks).

In spite of all these differences, the tradition of dialectical criticism, as we may call it, has exhibited a remarkable unity of method in its applications of general principles to the analysis of literary works. As with philological criticism, the basis of analysis has been consistently the ancient dichotomy of content and form; but with the absorption of the two terms into a dialectical system their status tends to undergo a striking change. They cease to be merely the distinguishable elements of any grammatically complete utterance and become dialectical opposites, the significance of which is determined by the general oppositions, whatever they may be, of the critic's scheme. Depending upon these, "content" in the sense of the psychological and moral tendencies of the author may be viewed as an internal principle, the

6

soul of the work, in relation to which the "form" is the external body (as in Louis Cazamian); or "form" may be thought of as internal and "content," in the sense of the raw materials of experience, as external (as in Walter Pater). Again, "form" as semantic "structure" may be made the essence of poetry, with "content" as only its paraphrastic statement (as in Cleanth Brooks); or the distinction may be reduced to one between "outer form" and "inner form" (as in Wellek and Warren's *Theory of Literature*); or "form" in poetry may be defined as what distinguishes poetry as synthetic from prose as analytic and "content" identified as social attitude and thus as extraliterary (as in F. W. Bateson); or "form" may be subordinated as concrete "present-ment" to "content" as the moral preoccupations that characterize a writer's "peculiar interest in life" and hence be incapable of judg-ment apart from these (as in F. R. Leavis). There is no need to give more examples, but we may note that much the same thing has hap-pened also, in this mode of criticism, to the originally Aristotelian "parts" of tragedy and epic; thus plot and character are often made dialectical contraries (as in E. M. Forster's book on the novel) and drama is sometimes divided into "drama," comprising plot, character, spectacle, and music, and "poetry," comprising diction and thought (as in some modern discussions of Shakespeare).

The same mode of reasoning has also been used in the derivation and definition of literary kinds. The status and character of these in the many systems of critical dialectic developed since antiquity have varied considerably. Depending upon the premises of the system, dis-tinctions of genre at times have assumed great importance (as in ear-lier neoclassical criticism) and at other times (as in Croce) have been banished from the realm of the esthetic altogether and treated merely as conveniences in the bibliographical description of works. They have represented for some critics (for example, Boileau) dis-tinctions fixed in the nature of things and for others (for example, Johnson) only man-made conventions. In some periods or schools of criticism the list of essentially different genres has been a long one; in others, especially since the eighteenth century, the number has been much reduced. There have been added, moreover, to the traditional genres of the ancient grammarians, many other kinds of differentia-tion, the principles of which depend similarly upon oppositions pe-culiar to the systems in which they appear: differentiations, in which the historical names take on the status of universals, between national or period styles—for example, Attic and Asiatic, French and English (especially for drama), Renaissance and Baroque, Classical and Romantic or Preromantic, Metaphysical and Augustan—or between the styles of individual artists, as when critics oppose the manner of Donne and that of Spenser, or speak of the Horatian, Juvenalian, and Varronian types of satire. Kinds have also been constituted, notably in modern criticism, on the model of dialectic itself; an example being Cleanth Brooks's distinction, following I. A. Richards and, more remotely, Coleridge, between two fundamental kinds of poetic "structure"—that characterized by "wit," that is, the union of naturally opposed impulses or attitudes (thought and emotion, the "poetic" and "non-poetic," the "noble" and "satiric") and that characterized by a "dissociation" of these attributes and a more or less exclusive concentration on one or other of the simple extremes.

The variations in theory have been far more numerous than these few instances will suggest, but the underlying method of definition has remained essentially the same. Distinctions of genre, for all these critics, are distinctions not among species of individual art objects or among historically determined conventions but among general qualities or complexes of qualities which are often identified as peculiarly characteristic of one or another of the recognized forms but not restricted to it. Thus terms like epic, tragedy, comedy, pastoral, lyric, and so on, can be used analogically to designate manifestations of a certain quality no matter in what different literary kinds they may appear; and this is even more obviously the case with such later generic terms as "metaphysical," "Augustan," "romantic," "sublime," "synthetic," and the like. It is inevitable, therefore, that the problem of defining kinds in any dialectical system in which it is important to do this should entail the setting up of general oppositions which will justify, on rational grounds, as distinct from a posteriori inductions, the differentiations the critic wishes to make. Hence the many attempts to discover natural foundations for the basic poetic kinds, sometimes by equating them with fixed differences in society, sometimes by resolving them into temperamental types, sometimes by relating them to elementary distinctions of grammar. Whatever the analogy chosen, the result has uniformly been some scheme of genres, more or less comprehensive, and often, though not always, involving

8

a hierarchical order, in which one kind of writing is set against another as its dialectical opposite (as when comedy is made on all points the contrary of tragedy, or "Spenserian" poetry of "metaphysical") or in which one kind is related to others as the whole of which they are but incomplete contrasting parts (as in the theories, already referred to, of Richards and Brooks).

The same rules of procedure, finally, have governed the selection of predicates for the characterization and discrimination of authors and works. The aim is to discover and formulate distinguishing qualities of mind and art, and given the method, the formulas constructed in any given case must depend quite as much upon the kinds of oppositions furnished by the critic's theory of poetry or literature (even if this is only a more or less coherent set of terminological habits) as upon the data supplied by his texts—what constitutes relevant data, indeed, being determined by the analogy on which the theory rests. This is of course the reason, quite apart from differences of sensibility or taste, why the same poem or poet tends to exhibit so many different characters in the pages of different critics or historians. Thus Johnson, thinking in terms of the general conditions of literary pleasure, finds the distinctive quality of *The Rape of the Lock* in the union by Pope of "the two most engaging powers of an author," that which makes new things familiar and that which makes familiar things new: the crucial aspect of the poem for him, therefore, is its depiction of characters and actions. A more recent critic, however, conceiving of poetry, in opposition to prose, as essentially metaphorical language, locates the peculiar achievement of Pope and the critical problem he presents, "in a very special kind of reconciliation between qualities of poetry and prose, a reconciliation managed even after the maximum concessions have been made": for him the crucial aspects of Pope's poetry lie not so much in its subjects or arguments as in its devices of imagery and expression. Wide as these differences have inevitably been, the method of practical criticism in this tradition has never greatly changed, from the chapters in Quintilian's *Institutes* on the Greek and Roman poets, historians, orators, and philosophers to the essays of T. S. Eliot on the seventeenth-century English poets. Its chief tools, as Eliot remarks, are comparison and analysis, and its operations consist in the joining and separating, by these means, of whatever general literary qualities the critic may think it important to distinguish in a work or, more typically, a writer. An excellent modern example is Eliot's essay on Andrew Marvell. This is too familiar to quote, but one passage, also on Marvell, may be cited from a contemporary historian as an illustration in brief of how the thing is done. Marvell, we are told,

> united in himself, with an independent moderation of his own, a fresh, muscular, agile, and subtle metaphysical wit and the rationality, clarity, economy, and structural sense of a genuine classic, the cultured, negligent grace of a cavalier and something of the religious and ethical seriousness of a Puritan Platonist. To this rare combination of gifts were added, moreover, a feeling for nature at once particular and general, earthly and unearthly, and an individual sensitivity and suppleness of rhythm. In some of these qualities, and in his response to the claims of both contemplative solitude and public affairs, Marvell had a degree of affinity with his friend Milton. . . . He owed of course a prime debt to Donne and Donne's disciples, perhaps a small one to such *libertins* as Saint-Amant, and some other tinctures in his elixir are implied in his praise of Lovelace and of Jonson. These classical and metaphysical, continental and English, epicurean and Puritan, civilized and simple elements are mingled in varying proportions in Marvell's poems and, except in his style, they are not always fused. The Christian and the Platonist are not very close to the passionate lover, nor the poet of gardens to the future political satirist.[1]

And the historian proceeds to manipulate these or other closely equivalent contraries in a series of characterizations of Marvell's principal poems.

It will be recognized, I think, that the critical elements of most literary histories have been constituted by one or the other of the two methods, philological and dialectical, which I have been attempting to describe, or by a combination of them. That they are both legitimate and fruitful methods of solving problems, I should not question. Like all methods in any field, both of them may suffer characteristic corruptions in the hands of incompetent practitioners: the corruption

[1] Douglas Bush, *English Literature in the Earlier Seventeenth Century* (vol. 5: "Oxford History of English Literature") (Oxford, 1945), p. 159.

of the first is typically some kind of antiquarian irrelevance; that of the second, random or irresponsible impressionism and the cult of metaphorical statement.

Valid as they are, however, both methods are necessarily limited in the kinds of propositions they permit the historian to make about literary works. Both are concerned with wholes as well as with parts (in different senses of the terms), but in neither is the whole the concrete whole of the individual literary work, determined peculiarly by the choices of the artist. For the philological critic the wholeness of a poem or drama is merely the grammatical completeness of any text; it is, from the point of view of the critic's inquiries, simply a fact which he is given, and his problems consequently center on the parts and entail historical solutions independent of inferences from the whole. For the dialectical critic such inferences are possible, but the primary wholes with which he is concerned are dialectical compositions of qualities inhering in the author as unifying source, with the result that what he is able to discriminate in works are, again, only the characteristics of parts.

And the two methods are limited in still another way. There are three general aspects in terms of which literary productions may be defined: the preconstructional aspect, as I shall call it, comprising the relations of works to their origins and sources, whether these are considered literally or analogically; the postconstructional aspect, comprising the effects of completed works on readers; and the constructional aspect, comprising the artistic principles and judgments operative in their composition. All three of these ought ideally to be taken account of by the historian, but in the two modes of analysis we have so far discussed only the first and the second can be accorded adequate treatment—and that by means of distinctions which inevitably remain general and causally remote from the unique combinations of traits that differentiate individual works.

These limitations can be overcome, doubtless at the expense of other disadvantages, by resort to a third mode of deriving critical predicates for works—that which rests upon what I may call the concept of artistic synthesis.

The ruling assumption of this critical mode is that poetry (as before, in the large sense of imaginative literature) is not distinctively a mode or quality of discourse or a species of knowledge, practical action, expression, communication, entertainment, myth, or the like (although all these things are involved in poetry); it is simply the art (more precisely, the collection of arts) of making individual dramas, lyric poems, novels, short stories, and so on. So considered, a literary work is a concrete whole, or synthesis of parts, of a certain kind, the generic character of which is determined by the fact that it is the product of an artist combining elements of speech, with its various possible rhythms, and elements of humanly interesting experience or thought, by means of devices of technique and arrangement, for the sake of a particular organizing effect or series of effects on our opinions, emotions, or behavior. It is a whole that produces its effect not instantaneously but gradually in order of time; and its parts are consequently of two sorts: sequential parts, from beginning through middle to end, and functional parts that depend on the specific nature of the elements combined in the synthesis and on the mode of their combination. In all works, and in all the temporal parts of any work, we may differentiate effects or problems that derive from the author's choice of medium (as prose or meter of some kind), from his constitution of his subject (as an argument or action or state of character or feeling), and from his selection of a particular manner of representation (as narrative or dramatic). These are the three necessary conditions of the existence of any literary work as a concrete whole and hence the three fundamental criteria by which works of various kinds may be distinguished. In any group of works selected for purposes of comparison, each of these elements may vary in its specific character independently of variation in the others. Thus it is an error of method, in this mode of criticism, to reduce them to any one of the three, as in the doctrine that a literary work is "a system of signs," or even to any two, as in the old dichotomy of content and form. All elements being essential, moreover, no one of them, as it functions in completed works, can be said to be "unliterary" or "esthetically indifferent." The three elements cannot be properly reduced or collapsed, but each of them may be further differentiated in the poetics of a given species of work: Aristotle, for instance, resolves the qualitative parts common to tragedy and epic into plot, character, thought, and diction.

These and similar distinctions have been dismissed as mere "abstractions" by critics more concerned with the responses of readers than with the conditions of success or failure in literary production. For the writer, however, they constitute distinct and real, though related, loci of problems. This can easily be seen if we consider that a playwright, for example, may begin by sketching his plot as a whole, with its constituent incidents and essential determinations of character and thought, in a continuous sequence of speeches, then, in subsequent rewritings, reconsider each of the speeches to see how it would properly go if the characters were specified further in such and such ways, then work through the whole again for the sake of getting a proper maximum of implication in the dialogue, and finally decide that it would be more effective and appropriate to substitute verse for his original prose or prose for his original verse. The critic may therefore take this possibility as the basis of his analysis of works, and his problem then is not merely to identify the peculiar qualities possessed by the parts (in either sense) of any work, but to consider how each part has been made to function in relation to the others and to the artistic whole which the poet has achieved. For the whole in any literary product viewed as a concrete object is, analytically speaking, something over and above the mere combination of its separately determinable elements; it is the form that synthesizes their diverse qualities and local functions in the temporal progression of the words. It is therefore, for the literary artist, a final end or first principle of construction, from which he infers, however instantaneously, what he must do in constituting and ordering the parts. And there must always be, in any well-constructed poem, drama, or novel, some one part (in tragedy, the plot) the form of which determines most completely the form or effect of the whole, whereas the other parts (in tragedy, character, thought, diction, and spectacle) exist in their particular determinations for the sake of it, however "finished" and interesting they may be in themselves.

When literary works are thus conceived, the center of critical attention is appropriately the various problems of object, means, and manner involved in their construction as artistic syntheses of this or that special kind. It is sometimes said that we must abandon the pretence that there are significantly distinguishable literary forms (as distinct from conventions) and consider every poem as presenting a unique set of problems to the poet who makes it and hence to the critic who attempts to say how it is made. It is of course a fact that the composition of each new poem raises questions and poses difficulties for its author which have never had to be faced before. If this were all, however—that is, if no universals were involved and each poem were to be considered completely sui generis—it is hard to see how we could react coherently to any poem or how poets could learn from one another or how any of the literary arts could develop. The truth is that the artistic problems which perplex any author engaged in constructing any new work become problems for him precisely because universals *are* involved. His task is to embody his new materials and insights in words that will be effective in a particular way on the minds of readers, and he cannot do this without being governed, however unconsciously, by what a contemporary novelist has called "rules of construction, mysterious relations in technique, which exist apparently in the nature of art itself, and which oblige the artist to respect them."[2] Some of these, and the problems they raise, are generic to all kinds of writing or to all kinds in which the principal part is (say) a plot (for example, problems of arousing emotion or of intimating character or of achieving suspense and surprise) or to all kinds in which the manner is (say) narrative rather than dramatic. But some of them—and these are the most immediately compelling—are determined for the artist specifically by the principle of construction operative in his work but not unique to it, in the sense that other works having the same principle but a different matter can obviously be written (for example, other novels evoking the same kinds of emotion in the same sequence as *Emma* or *Persuasion*). In the composition of any work aspiring to a high degree of artistic integration there can be no final solutions of the general problems of writing apart from solution of the problems arising from the fact that certain concrete materials are to be given a certain specific form. That is to say, problems of style or the problems of writing, perhaps, a poetic drama cannot be solved independently of the problems the author faces in giving certain materials of his own invention a specific (and hence definable) form, or power—that of a tragedy like *The Duchess of Malfi,* for instance, rather than that of a tragedy like *Othello* or of one like *Venice Preserved.*

2 Joyce Cary, as quoted by Crane, *The Languages of Criticism and the Structure of Poetry* (Toronto, 1953), p. 143.

We can properly continue to talk, therefore, of literary forms, meaning by the term not traditional genres like "epistle," "ode," or "ballad opera," or constructed subject-matter classes like "revenge tragedy" or "graveyard poetry," or any of the many dialectically derived literary types such as "the poetry of synthesis," but species of works, inductively known, and differentiated, more or less sharply, in terms of their peculiar artistic elements and principles of construction. When the term "form" is so taken, distinctions of literary kind may range from the broad distinction between imitative and didactic forms (necessarily implying many subordinate differences in such things as plot, character, thought, and language), through distinctions based on some specific determination of either means, manner, or object (for example, that between recitative, declamatory, and fully mimetic drama), to the most completely formal distinctions, involving specifications of object, means, manner, and effect in some particular causal ordering, of which Aristotle's definition of tragedy in *Poetics* 6, as limited still further by *Poetics* 13 and 14, is the classic example.

From all this two important corollaries follow. In the first place, the principles which differentiate kinds of literary works in this analysis are obviously poetic ends, but their status as such is very different from that of the variously derived ends of poetry or of particular species of poetry in the two other modes of criticism. They are not ends in the sense either of historically known intentions of writers in composing particular works (as when we say, for instance, that Fielding intended *Joseph Andrews* to be a comic romance "in the manner of Cervantes") or of ideal ends dialectically deduced from premises concerning the nature of poetry and its relation to other arts and activities (as in the numerous variations on the *aut prodesse aut delectare* of Horace). Rather, they are ends induced from the history of literature by analysis of the final causes which have actually determined, and therefore can still determine, the production of literary works. We know thus that poems can be written for the sake of inculcating knowledge or of persuading readers to or against some mode of moral or political action, and we also know that writers may go beyond such practical purposes and compose poems of which the ends are the peculiar pleasures afforded by their beautiful and moving representations of different forms of human experience. We know further that

15

when this happens, the imitative ends can subsume, without suppressing, the more general practical aims, so that we can say, with a modern critic, that all art is propaganda though not all propaganda is art. And we know, finally, that after specifically different forms have come into existence and been elaborated in all their parts for imitative purposes, the same forms, or rather the rules and devices they have made available to writers, may again be subordinated to constructive principles of a didactic order (as has happened in our time to many of the highly developed species of fiction, lyric poetry, and drama). For the critic in this mode, consequently, there can be no such thing as "true poetry" or the "ideal" tragedy or novel; his first business, whatever else he may do, is to consider literary works, without prejudice, in the light of the specific ends or principles of construction, whatever they may be, which have in fact, on the best hypothesis he can form, governed their composition and of the theoretically known conditions of maximum excellence peculiar to each.

And the second corollary is a variant of this: it is the all-importance of distinctions of literary species, in the meaning here given that term, to the critic of individual works. For on the assumption, which is basic to criticism of this sort, that no artist, as Eliot has said, "produces great art by a deliberate attempt to express his personality"—he "expresses his personality indirectly through concentrating upon a task which is a task in the same sense as the making of an efficient engine or the turning of a jug or table-leg"—the primary judgments of the critic must clearly be judgments of how well, in terms of its specific requirements, the poet's task has been performed: that is to say, he will make judgments in kind. He will not think of reproaching Milton, in *Lycidas* or *Paradise Lost,* for failing to write like Donne without first asking whether these poems would have been better for the same handling of language and verse as the *Satyres.* In short, he will begin by inquiring, for any work he intends to consider, what its peculiar species is; not for the sake of debating how far it has realized the ideal form of this species, but rather for the sake of knowing what particular criteria are relevant to the analysis or criticism of its parts. Thus he will avoid, for example, the error of judging *The Duchess of Malfi* as if it were a tragedy of the same species as *Othello,* or of discussing the merits and faults of *Murder in the Cathedral* as if it were a drama of a traditional sort rather than a special modern kind of lyric poem, or of treating all great poems, novels, and dramas, whether constructed as imitations or not, as if they were allegories or myths.

It should be easy now to see what must be the critical equipment of the historian who proposes to deal with literary productions, of whatever period, in terms of the concept of artistic synthesis. His first aim must be to achieve a maximum of *artistic* particularity and relevance in his statements about the traits of individual works or historical groupings of works. His procedure is dictated, in its main lines, by the fact that literary works may differ from one another, artistically, both with respect to the character of the whole which the writer has achieved, more or less successfully, in each and with respect to the nature and handling of their parts. The historian's account of any work will not be complete unless it includes specifications concerning both aspects, and the terms in which these can appropriately be couched will necessarily differ according as, for example, the work is imitative or didactic (a "plot" is not at all the same sort of thing as an allegorical fable) or as its subject is an extended action or a concentrated manifestation of feeling, thought, or moral choice. In all cases, however, the primary problem is that of the specific nature of the whole, and it is adequately solved only when this is stated formally—that is, as a principle of construction ordering the concrete materials of incident, character, thought, imagery, and the like—and in such a way as to permit us to distinguish the particular problems which the writer faced as a consequence of his choice of form. The form or effect of any work depends immediately, as we have seen, upon the form of its principal part, whether this is a plot form of one kind or another or something else having a similar architectonic function. This must be analyzed, as precisely as is possible or useful for the historian's purpose, in terms of its distinctive organization and intended effect on the thoughts and emotions of readers. (For a simple example see below, pp. 283 ff.) The problem of the parts is secondary, but not therefore, for the historian, any less important, inasmuch as in any group of works having the same essential form there may be radical differences in the treatment of its characteristic qualitative elements, depending in part upon the special character of the writer's material *données* or of his extraformal ends, in part upon his special choices of technique. Instances of the first sort of difference are the relatively slight magnitude of the action in *Coriolanus* as compared with Shakespeare's other tragedies and the relatively greater development of its thought over its plot and character; and, again, as between *Cymbeline* and *Philaster*—both tragicomedies of much the same species—the much completer subordination in Shakespeare's play as compared with Fletcher's of the particular scenes to the demands of the overall form. These are relevant observations for the historian of literature if only because they—and the innumerable similar observations that may be made on other works—present causal problems of a peculiarly literary kind. And the same thing is true of the differences he must observe in his writers' uses of traditional or novel devices of technique —both dictional and representational—in relation to such formal ends as depicting character, externalizing thought, or making the activity represented in the work seem probable, important, or emotionally effective in proper degree.

The task of analysis, at least for the works that are to be given special prominence in a history, is thus not simple, and its performance can easily be vitiated by one or another of the faults of method which constitute the characteristic corruptions of this critical mode. One of these is "formalism," or the disposition to reduce problems of artistic form to questions of "structure" merely, in abstraction from the humanly interesting and moving aspects of works upon which their form in the full sense of its peculiar moral and emotional quality essentially depends. Corruption also results from the confusion of artistic principles with techniques, from the substitution of a conception of literary kinds as "norms" for the conception of them as first principles of construction, and finally, and perhaps most disastrously, from the natural tendency to force individual works into formal molds that are either inappropriate to them (as when the *Essay on Criticism* is read as an instance of theoretical rather than practical or moral argument) or too rigid or generalized in definition to fit their peculiar characteristics (as in all discussions of tragic or tragicomic or comic plays and novels which neglect to consider these terms as embracing a considerable variety of distinctive plot forms).

Against such errors, given a historian with some sensitivity to differences of literary effect, the necessary safeguards are of two sorts. The first is experience: whatever his period of specialization, it will be better if he has read widely and critically in works of all kinds written in other periods and languages, especially those which exhibit the sharpest contrasts in the species of literature cultivated and in the character of the preferred techniques. Acquaintance with the ancients is thus indispensable for intelligent work in any modern period, and sympathetic knowledge of contemporary literature, particularly in its more revolutionary and experimental aspects, is essential for any properly discriminating study of the past. It will be better also if the historian has himself written or attempted to write poems or novels—and has meditated on the varieties of problems they present. The second safeguard is an adequate grounding in the theory on which this method of analysis depends. This will include both an understanding of its underlying assumptions about the nature of poetry and criticism and a constantly increasing set of critical tools. The latter are inductively tested differentiae for discriminating, literally and appropriately, the forms of works, distinguishing their parts and the varied functions they serve, and particularizing among their technical devices with respect both to the constitution of these and the specific uses to which they are put.

If it is asked where such an apparatus may be obtained, the answer must be, I think, that it exists as yet only in fragments. The *Poetics*, for all its limitations, is still an essential text, useful for its analysis of one species of tragedy, for its indications of criteria for the general consideration of plot, character, thought, diction, narrative manner, and the like, in imitative works, and, most important, for its exemplification of the methods of analysis and reasoning requisite to a literal inquiry into poetic works viewed concretely as products of different poetic arts. The historian can learn much, also, from the scattered remarks of poets and other creative writers, from Dante to Henry James, on the artistic and technical problems they faced in their works; a comprehensive list of references to these, indexed according to the questions at issue, would be an invaluable tool. But there is clearly much theoretical work still to be done. This could profitably include, for one thing, a systematic reconsideration of the devices of literary language—both the familiar devices codified in the older traditions of rhetoric and the newer devices invented by modern novelists and poets—from the point of view of their possible functions relative to poetic ends. It could very well include also an attempt to reduce to greater analytical precision such fashionable but extremely vague

19

concepts as "symbolism," "pattern," and "myth." What is chiefly needed, however, is the inductive development of distinctions sufficiently numerous and refined to permit us to deal more accurately than we now can with modes of artistic synthesis of which Aristotle took no account. These modes include, for example, various forms of imitative drama and narrative intermediate between tragedy and comedy, the numerous shorter forms commonly referred to loosely as "lyric poems" and "short stories," and the many poetic species which are organized by extrinsic principles rather than by principles intrinsic to their matter, such as Ibsen's *Ghosts,* Orwell's *Animal Farm,* or C. P. Snow's *The Masters.*

To define the artistic particularity of works in the light of such relevant poetic theory as may be available is, then, the first task of the historian in this mode. It is not, however, his only task, since the peculiar effect and significance of individual poems, novels, and dramas is obviously a function not only of their formal constitution (although it is primarily a function of this), but likewise of two other factors which the historian can hardly neglect.

The first of these is the nature of the *données* which the writer has drawn from his experience, reflection, or reading and ordered to one poetic end or another in his work. It is not a matter of indifference, for contemporary readers at least and hence for the historian, whether the locales of plays and narratives are domestic or foreign, near or remote in time, familiar or novel; or whether their characters are depicted in ordinary or extraordinary people, acting and thinking according to a generally received code of morals and manners or according to one considered "advanced" for the time; or whether the events represented are such as may occur normally to any man in a given society or such as happen only rarely or in circumstances of a special sort or such as are impossible except to the imagination; or whether the "thought" of a work is derived from common and popular opinion or from some system of science or philosophy; or whether the stock of imagery from which a lyric poet (or novelist or playwright) draws is large or small, secondhand or original, traditional to a certain kind of poetry or "modern" and new, organized in a coherent set of myths (as in Yeats) or existing only as discrete parts; or whether the writer's language is selective or inclusive, old-fashioned or current, literary or conversational; and so on. These are all distinctions of a material order, such as a merely philological criticism is competent to investigate. They bear directly upon the task of the historian concerned with works as artistic syntheses, however: they signify differences which determine to some degree expectations and probabilities in plots and lyric poems and so inevitably qualify the effects of various works having the same formal principle; and differences of these kinds have often constituted the matter of significant or even revolutionary changes in literary practice. For these reasons the historian of the literary arts must unite statements concerning them with his propositions about the more purely formal aspects of the works he examines; he must take pains, however, to order and interpret all such material or conventional traits in the light of his poetic distinctions.

The second factor is the nature of the writer's mind. Here the historian will be involved with characteristics of literary works, over and above their distinguishing formal and material attributes, which enable him to say, for example, of various works by a single writer, that they are products of a naive or sophisticated mind; of a mind disposed to reduce experience and moral issues to simple oppositions or of one consistently impressed by the complexities of things; of a pioneering or iconoclastic mind or of one inclined to build upon, while transcending, the intellectual or literary past; of a mind dominated by limited interests or of one given to a wide-ranging concern with the problems of his time. It is needless to argue that the degree of pleasure afforded by different works and the seriousness with which mature readers can regard them are strongly influenced by such considerations. They are the sort of considerations that have motivated the many attempts of critics in the qualitative tradition to state the conditions of "greatness" in literature, either generally (as in Longinus) or particularly (as in the essays of Matthew Arnold or, more recently, in books like Eliot's *After Strange Gods* and Leavis' *The Great Tradition*). The historian must accordingly take differences of this kind into account in formulating his characterizations of works; the only difficulty is that they lend themselves more easily to dialectical or metaphorical statement or to some species of biographical, psychological, or doctrinal reduction than to literal definition in terms of the analyzable elements of thought, feeling, and diction through which they are realized in particular dramas, novels, and poems. Of all the theorists who have occupied themselves with the problem, only

Longinus, perhaps, saw clearly what a causal and problematic inquiry into qualities, as general qualities of literature, might be; and what seems to be needed, therefore, if the historian of literary forms is to combine coherently with his other judgments of works judgments concerning the moral and literary personalities reflected in them, is a modern development and extension of the art devised by Longinus for the attainment of the "sublime."

It is clear that both these factors, though in different ways, are related to what may be called the preconstructional and postconstructional aspects of a literary work—that is, with what precedes and what follows the shaping of the writer's materials into *this* individual production. It is, however, with the aspects of the work as thus constructed—its constructional aspects—that the historian who bases his analyses on the concept of artistic synthesis is primarily concerned, and he must consequently seek to frame his elementary propositions about works in such a way as to bring these other aspects into causal connection with the aspects defined by his poetic theory. The solution of this problem depends upon the solution of another problem, even more fundamental. This problem is posed by the fact that although literary works in any critical view are essentially objects of contemplation, the values of which as finished products of art are analytically separable from the processes of their composition and hence not resolvable into history, the literary historian is necessarily committed to regarding such works *sub specie temporis,* in relation to the careers, interests, and environing circumstances of their writers. The problem may be solved in a variety of ways, but the solution most consonant with the premises of this third mode of criticism is one that consists in taking the concrete wholeness of a work as the proximate end of its author's productive activity and reasoning back from what the work is, as an object of critical analysis, to the particular problems and decisions—defined artistically rather than psychologically—which its production entailed, and thence to the particular materials and qualities of mind which set the conditions in which the author's choices of form and of formative devices took place. It is only, indeed, by such a translation of products into processes that the historian in this mode can bridge the gap between the two kinds of statement which, as we saw in the beginning, all literary historians have to make and compose a history which will be a history of forms as well as of writers and deal

22

with the artistic uses made of materials and conventions as well as with the historical causes that brought these into vogue and determined their character and appeal.

2. PRINCIPLES OF ORGANIZATION

The minimum principles of organization of any literary history are obviously succession in time, distribution in space (which we need not consider here), and likeness and difference in character. When these principles alone are operative, unmodified by others, the result will be what for lack of a better word may be called *atomistic history*. Among the innumerable histories, ancient and modern, which belong to this species by virtue at least of their general construction, it will suffice to mention the historical chapters in Quintilian's *Institutes*, Joseph Spence's pioneer account of the English poets, Johnson's *Lives*, Warton's *History of English Poetry*, the *Histoire littéraire de la France*, Hallam's *Introduction to the Literature of Europe*, Stopford Brooke's *Primer of English Literature*, the Petit de Julleville history of French literature, the Cambridge histories, the first part of Legouis and Cazamian's history, and the volumes thus far published in the Oxford history; a complete list would include a majority of the histories, comprehensive or selective, erudite or popular, which have undertaken to survey systematically the literary productions of a nation, an age, or a class of writers.

In all these the primary units of interpretation are either works or, more commonly, authors viewed as the most immediate cause of the characteristics exhibited by their works, but the individual histories differ widely according to the fashion in which the basic principles of succession and of likeness and difference are construed. The minimal extreme in this respect is perhaps best represented by the *Histoire littéraire*, especially in the volumes edited and in part written by Charles-Victor Langlois: here the comparison is conducted in the strictest philological terms, and the primary succession is of individual writers or anonymous works (the latter occasionally grouped in subject-matter classes) ordered solely by their known or conjectured dates without partition into periods. This is too austere an ideal, however, to have satisfied many historians of this type. At the very least, even among those whose conception of criticism has remained predominantly philological, it has appeared necessary to classify the authors dealt with, or all except the most eminent, in terms of some particular criterion, or combination of criteria, of likeness and difference. The most common determinant has been the literary genre to which the major efforts of a given writer were devoted—as in the familiar divisions into writers of verse and writers of prose; dramatists, novelists, poets, essayists, and critics; tragic dramatists and comic dramatists; religious poets and secular poets; poets of the town and poets of the country. These distinctions have usually been combined, however, in either a subordinating or a subordinate relation, with other kinds of distinctions. At times these have been based on the personal, professional, social, political, or ideological affinities of writers—as, for instance, Pope and his friends as distinct from the group surrounding Addison or Johnson and his circle; amateur writers and writers who lived by their pens; clerical and lay writers or middle-class and aristocratic writers; Whig writers and Tory writers; orthodox writers and deists. At other times such distinctions have been based on the traditions of matter or manner writers professed to follow as the disciples of Spenser, Jonson, and Donne; or on the characters of the audiences they wrote for as courtly and popular dramatists; or on their preferred modes of publication as anthologists, pamphleteers, or journalists. The temporal succession of writers is also broken, in most histories of this type, by divisions into periods or ages, the definitions of which are sometimes drawn merely from the calendar (as in Hallam, whose story from 1500 on begins afresh every fifty years), sometimes from changes of rulers or other political transformations, sometimes from phases in the general history of culture (for example, the Middle Ages, the Renaissance, the Enlightenment), and frequently, as in many "survey" histories of the standard sort, from an eclectic mixture of these and other similarly external criteria.

Beyond this only one further step is possible without abandonment of the principle of atomistic succession on which these histories are based. This step is taken whenever historians, not content with an exclusively philological approach, resort to one of the numerous varieties of qualitative criticism in their comparisons of writers and works. The succession still remains one primarily of writers, whether these are considered separately, one after the other, as in Johnson's *Lives* (which typifies the minimal extreme of this mode) or are grouped according to one or more of the classifying devices just mentioned; but the writers are no longer treated merely as authors of such and such works exhibiting such and such material traits of content and form as a result of the circumstances of their origin, but as exponents, in varying combinations and degrees of completeness, of the "values" which the historian demands in poetry or literature generally or those which he thinks distinctive of the age. The history thus becomes a record of successive manifestations of literary characteristics—those of individual writers in the first place, but those also, at least in most histories written since the middle of the eighteenth century, of schools of writers, traditions, movements, tendencies, periods. And as these can be defined and related to one another only in terms of some pattern of dialectical distinctions and oppositions (the historian having no causal theory of literary kinds to supply him with variables and unifying ends of a more literal sort), the parts of the history, from its statements about authors and their works to its statements about schools, traditions, and ages, tend to display those traits of organization which we have already seen to be consequential on this method. If there is to be ordering of qualities at all, its basis, in any particular context, must be a single principle of division under which all the more specific distinctions the historian may hit upon can be subsumed. Hence the frequency, in such histories, of sharp and schematic contrasts between writers, schools, traditions, or periods considered en bloc, as when Ben Jonson's poetry is opposed as a whole to the poetry, similarly unified, of Donne; or as when, in like fashion, the "line of wit" (which now includes both Jonson and Donne) is set over against the "line" which runs from Spenser through Milton and his eighteenth-century imitators to Keats and Tennyson; or as when in numerous histories and in terms of many different criteria of division, the literature of the Restoration and early eighteenth century is defined in antithesis to that of the Renaissance, or the Romantic period differentiated, by a series of compendent contrarieties, from the preceding Neoclassic age.

Such single-principled oppositions of authors and of large or small groupings of authors have become so familiar in literary historiography that we tend to think of them as generalizations of the same order as those made by a military or political historian when

25

he distinguishes between the generalship of Lee and that of Grant or between the Old and the New Whigs in the 1790's or between the social state of England before and after the Industrial Revolution. In fact, however, they are generalizations of a very different kind, resting not upon a matter-of-fact causal analysis of events in terms peculiarly appropriate to the nature of the phenomena—military, political, economic, and so on—which happen to be in question, but upon what Hume called "relations of ideas," that is, general abstract distinctions applicable to many or all kinds of things. In other words, the qualitative particulars to be discriminated, are taken in abstraction from their immediate literary causes or reasons in individual works and interpreted as instances or manifestations of one or another of the metaphysical contrarieties or dialectical commonplaces which constitute the historian's analytical stock in trade. The differences between Wordsworth and Shelley are thus resolved, in F. R. Leavis' history, into two contrasting relations between thought and feeling and two contrasting attitudes toward tradition. In Hallam the distinctions among schools of English poetry in the early seventeenth century are derived from a basic schematism of the mental faculties—imagination, reason, and emotion—which for him ultimately determine all literary effects. In Stopford Brooke's *Primer,* the history of poetic style from 1600 to 1800 is reduced to a series of permutations of those familiar terms of all work, "nature" and "art." In Paul Van Tieghem's book on the Romantic movement in Europe, the major division of Romantic subject matter, which is then used to organize the accounts of Romantic poetry and Romantic fiction, is based on the even more general distinction of internal and external. And in *The Great Chain of Being,* A. O. Lovejoy has brilliantly subsumed the differences between the so-called Romantic period and the Enlightenment, in both subject matter and style, under the simple antithesis—which may serve to organize many other histories besides—of a liking for diversity and a craving for the uniform and simple.

It is only to be expected that different histories of this type, though dealing with the same period or literature, should exhibit a remarkable variety of divergent classifications, emphases, and interpretations. Many of these, of course, are the natural result either of progress in scholarly discovery and proof or of changes in literary taste (so

26

that the judgments on many writers in the histories of a generation ago now seem comically dated); others merely reflect different notions of what the term "literature" properly includes. All these are fruitful sources of polemic among historians or between historians and their reviewers, but they are less relevant to our theme than are the differences which originate in the many possibilities of variation implicit in the method itself. Thus there are few histories in this tradition that do not combine the results of philological and biographical research with their dialectical characterizations and estimates; but individual histories differ greatly according as one or the other of the two elements is made to predominate and according as the two are more or less closely related in the historian's exposition. There are few histories, also, in which statements designed to show what each author had "by distinction" are not supplemented by statements designed to show what all the authors included or all the authors belonging to a particular group had in common; but here again in practice the extremes lie far apart. There are likewise few histories employing dialectical principles which do not allow the historian to mingle propositions about the historical "values" of his authors with propositions about their "values" in terms of some universal scale; but in this respect, too, the diversity is very great. And, lastly, although there are few histories of this type which do not treat in some fashion of both content and form in their descriptions and generalizations, the widest differences prevail with respect to the relative emphasis placed on the two aspects and with respect to the conceptions entertained by the historian of the nature of each and of its relation to the other.

Out of these divergences innumerable controversies have sprung, in which partisans of philology, or "history" pure and simple, have been ranged against critics; biographical and psychological critics against "historical" critics; "absolutist" critics against "relativist" critics; "formalist" critics against those who find the values of literature in its moral or sociological implications; and so on. In the nature of things no easy resolution of any of these disputes is possible, since all of them turn on the dogmatic opposition of half-truths; but that is not to say that there are no criteria for appraising the species of literary history which has given rise to the quarrels. That better and worse histories of this kind can be written is clear enough: they will be better, obviously, in proportion as the historian uses and makes available to others the findings of the best scholarship on the topics he treats and in proportion as he is himself an original and perceptive critic in the qualitative mode; who can be other than grateful for comprehensive and well-arranged repertories of information about literature and for fresh literary judgments on authors of the past? When this is said, however, we must admit that something is wanting in histories of literature conceived and organized as these are. They have all the limitations of the two modes of criticism on which their propositions are based, and in addition, as every one knows who has tried his hand at constructing one of them, if only in class lectures, they are very hard to do well, for two main reasons. In the first place, given only the principles of succession and of likeness and difference, the historian must perforce fall back on extrinsic criteria of relevance for determining what things or even what kinds of things he ought to say. He may aim at the ideal of bio-bibliographical completeness which has inspired the editors of the *Histoire littéraire*, but short of this his only guides in the selection of authors to be included, in the proportioning of space to these, in the elaboration or suppression of biographical, bibliographical, and other circumstantial details, and even in the choice of topics of qualitative characterization are such vague and arbitrary standards as those set by his private interests, theories, and tastes, the current fashions in scholarship and criticism, or the custom of the trade. And for the same reasons, secondly, there can be, in histories of this type, no principle of historical continuity of a more specific kind than the general persistence throughout the ages treated of a more or less widespread impulse to compose works of the various sorts included in the historian's definition of literature or poetry. They are necessarily wanting, therefore, in the dynamic quality which the best histories of political or military affairs have always had. The structure of the narrative, if it can be said to be a narrative structure at all, is distinguished by perpetual fresh starts—with each new period or subperiod, with each new topical division of a period, even with each new author; and the historian is compelled to exert all his dialectical or literary ingenuity in devising transitions from one large or small part to the next which will not betray too obviously the static character of his construction.

These difficulties have been felt by many literary historians as keenly as by most of their readers, and two principal efforts—sharply opposed in their conceptions of method—have been made to go beyond the simple principle of atomistic succession which has been chiefly responsible for the trouble.

One of these, based on an extension to the history as a whole of the devices of dialectical organization which we have seen operating in subordinate parts of the histories just considered has led to what may be called integral or organic literary history. The integration has been effected in a great many ways and in terms of many varying or conflicting theories of the nature of literature and of the connections between literature and other things. Sometimes these connections have been largely suppressed or relegated to a secondary or incidental rule, with the result that unity is achieved by the application to successive writers of a single dialectic of combination and separation having as its elements a compendent set of "literary" qualities or values, the necessity pervading the history being that of the disjunctive major premise of critical theory which holds it together. Examples of this are some of Eliot's early essays (especially those dealing with the progress from the seventeenth century to the nineteenth of the celebrated "dissociation of sensibility"), Leavis' *Revaluation* (which has a similar theme but with more intrusions of the social correlatives of the poetic traditions), and Cleanth Brooks's "Notes for a revised History of English Poetry" (composed, he tells us, in the belief that "the orthodox histories . . . will have to be rewritten . . . with more consistency than they now possess, and with emphasis on a more vital conception of the nature of poetry than that which now underlies them"). To this general class belongs also the conception of literary history expounded and exemplified by René Wellek, although the dialectical mechanism Wellek prefers to use is quite different. He too proposes a history which will be a history of literature "as literature and not another thing," as free from dependence on external factors as histories of music and painting have commonly been; and he insists that such a history can be written without treating literary development either as a meaningless flux, a mere series of differentiated works, or as a reflection of some absolute value "extraneous to the process of literature." His solution depends upon an analogy of literature to language as this is interpreted in the theories of the Genevan School and the Prague Linguistic Circle; it consists in "relating the historical process to a value or norm"—that is, a system of standards and conventions—which stands platonically as the One to the Many given by the historian's observations of particular writers and works (that is, it determines the common predicates to be applied to the latter) while being itself subject to change. By means of such a normative idea, which will differ from one historical context to another, we may constitute integrally, in exclusively "literary" terms, the history of an author, a literary genre, a period or movement, a national literature (even though this is "harder to envisage"), or an international literary development.

More frequently, however, the emphasis in the integrating dialectic has been on the other things with which literature in its general evolution, or in a particular phase of this, has been thought to be connected in a peculiarly intimate way. The simplest class of such histories consists of those in which writers or works are characterized in terms of their varying "expressions" or "reflections" of some single situation or line of development—sometimes described in a relatively literal fashion, sometimes simplified into a historical myth —in the general life of the time. There are many partial exemplifications of this device in histories based generally on the principle of atomistic succession (for instance, in Legouis' chapters on English poetry between 1580 and 1660) and, as every one knows, it has been often used, especially since the beginning of the nineteenth century, to organize whole histories, of a considerable variety of types, in which likenesses and differences among writers and works are defined primarily, though not always exclusively, by "correspondence" or "equation" with characteristics attributed to the unifying state of affairs or process of change. The latter has sometimes been conceived broadly as the shifting temper of a nation, as in Barrett Wendell's *The Temper of the Seventeenth Century in English Literature,* or, more specifically, as this temper modified by the circumstances of a new environment, as in Moses Coit Tyler's history of literature in colonial America. The unity, again, has sometimes been found in the continuity of political development, as in W. J. Courthope's *History of English Poetry* (based, as the preface informs us, on the postulate that the study of English poetry is in effect "the study of the continuous growth of our national institutions as reflected in our literature"); sometimes in the persistent opposition, in a given society, of antithetical political ideals, as in Virgil Parrington's history; sometimes in the manifestations of contemporary economic life, as in L. C. Knights's *Drama and Society in the Age of Jonson;* sometimes in the "moral history" of a people in a period of cultural crisis, as in Alfred Kazin's *On Native Grounds* (in which American writing between 1890 and 1940 is interpreted—but without neglect of its artistic traits—in relation to the widely felt need, created by the "moral transformation of our American life, thought, and manners under the impact of industrial capitalism and science," to learn "what the reality of life was in the modern era"); sometimes in the pattern of contemporary intellectual activity, as Sir Herbert Grierson's *Cross Currents in English Literature of the Seventeenth Century* (in which the literature is discussed as "reflecting the spiritual conflicts" of the age); sometimes in the evolution of the language, as in F. W. Bateson's *English Poetry and the English Language.* All these histories—and the many others that could be added to the list—are in their varying fashions dominated by a concern with "the relation between literary modes and ways of thinking and feeling, between quality of writing and quality of living"; it is the peculiar paradox, however, of their dialectical method that in proportion as they clarify "the ways of thinking and feeling" mirrored in their authors, the particularity of "the literary modes" tends to be obscured or reduced to a common denominator or political, social, intellectual, or linguistic terms. Their characteristic limitation is therefore the opposite of that inherent in the "literary" histories of Brooks and Wellek: just as those histories have the effect of unduly separating poetry from life, so these run the risk of unduly collapsing the history of poetry or literature into the "moral" history of the society it reflects.

The necessity present in such histories derives typically from the assumption that literary works must inevitably be mirrors of their age as well as, more immediately, of their authors' experiences and minds. This assumption underlies also another important group of modern literary histories, which differ, however, from those just considered by introducing another level of necessity—and hence of schematic integration—in the form of a dialectical analysis of the

31

underlying causal factors. The primary determinant has sometimes been the economic or political structure of society, as in the many attempts to write the history of literature in terms of Marxist theory or some variant thereof; an example, with special features of its own, is Bateson's *English Poetry: A Critical Introduction,* in which the major schools of English poetry are reduced to five (with a sixth not treated in detail), each with its "basic form of poetic statement" which is the "reflection" in its poetry of the peculiar character or "dominant incentive" of the contemporary "social order"; there have been five such orders from Chaucer's time to the present, the distinctive character of each being determined by a permutation of two pairs of contraries—collectivist and individualist, rural and urban. More commonly, however, the ultimate unifying causes have been given a psychological status in the common faculties or impulses of the mind; as, for example, in Taine's *History of English Literature,* in which all historical phenomena, including literature, are deduced from the operations of the understanding and the will as modified in the lapse of time by the three factors of *race, milieu,* and *moment;* or in Louis Cazamian's account of English literature from 1660 to the present, in which the literary evolution is plotted in terms of a necessary alternation of phases dominated by intelligence with phases dominated by imagination and feeling; or in Leslie Stephen's *History of English Thought in the Eighteenth Century,* in which a complicated dialectic of historical progress is built out of similar basic contraries; or, most recently, in Hiram Haydn's *The Counter Renaissance,* in which the distinction of two types of temperament— that which "believes in the essential congruence and relatedness of the ideal and the empirically actual" and that which sees only an irreconcilable discrepancy between the two—is used to schematize the whole intellectual and literary development, in England and on the Continent, between the later Middle Ages and the period of Newton. In the lengths to which they carry the principle of dialectical integration, these histories, it is evident, go far beyond any of the other varieties of this type of construction, and in doing so they encounter the characteristic danger, not only that the individual and specific traits of the literature will be submerged in the abstractions of the unifying scheme, but that the history itself will take on the

32

character not so much of history as of philosophy and so be judged as good or bad in terms of its dialectical adequacy alone.

There can be no doubt, however, that these various modes of organic history do achieve a solution of the twin problems of continuity and relevance posed by literary histories of the traditional atomistic kind: of the first by substituting a logical progression or schematism of ideas for simple chronological succession; of the second by providing a matrix of common terms and distinctions capable of being applied analogically to all writers and all species of works. The attractions of the method for such minds as tend to identify intelligibility in history with a reduction of its multifarious particulars to some principle of unity can readily be understood; the difficulty is that there are and have always been other minds, no less concerned with making sense out of the literary past, for whom any such dialectical reduction is bound to seem at once too easy and too destructive of the observable literal distinctness of works and of the reasons thereof to hold their interest for any length of time.

It is from historians of this latter kind that the second major solution of the problems of continuity and relevance in literary history has proceeded. Its model has been not dialectic but the narrative-causal sequences characteristic of those histories of political or military events which have developed beyond the stage of annals. And its principles, which determine the variety and interrelation of the propositions the historian has to make, are the general factors implicit in any concrete instance of change, of whatever sort, in nature or human affairs. These are: (1) an initial situation from which the change proceeds; (2) a final situation in which the first situation eventuates and which contrasts with the first in kind, quality, or amount; (3) a continuing matter which undergoes change and of which both end terms can be predicated; and (4) a moving cause, or convergence of moving causes, capable of bringing about the particular change defined by the other variables.

The possibility of constructing a literary history according to these principles depends, in the first place, upon the discovery, in any succession of works with which the historian may be concerned, of a continuing subject of change that can be stated in more or less specific and literal terms. (1) This may be interest in a particular

33

subject matter, myth, or body of doctrine which writers continue to exploit (as the world of natural phenomena, the Arthurian legends, the conception of romantic love); (2) it may be a special technique or type of medium to which successive writers devote themselves (as the writing of novels in letter form, the use of symbolic devices of representation, the heroic couplet); (3) it may be an established model, or corpus of similar models, which persists as an effective tradition (as the early poems of Milton, the comedies of Terence, the Cervantean manner in fiction, the prose style of Seneca); (4) it may be a particular genre, the conventions and rules of which continue to be used as a norm in creation (as dream allegory, drawing-room comedy, the verse tale, the detective novel, the Western story); (5) it may be a specific end or artistic problem which, once it has emerged, continues to direct literary practices (as writing poems in the service of religion, composing tragedies that will move the tender affections, devising meters suitable to drama, giving a lifelike quality to dialogue in fiction); or (6) it may be simply the persistence of a general desire, for example, to use language imitatively or to prevent drama, fiction, or poetry from degenerating into fixed routines with little immediate relevance to contemporary life.

The continuum of a narrative history may be drawn from any one of these, and the form of the change it sets forth is then constituted by taking as the initial and terminal points any more or less contrary sets of literary characteristics, exhibited successively by the works under consideration, that involve differences in the practice of writers which can be related causally to whatever is taken as the constant factor in the development. The differences thus may be differences of kind or form relative to the persistence of a given subject matter, technique, model of imitation, convention, problem, or general end, or they may be differences of quality in subject matter or technique relative to the continued cultivation of a given form, or they may be differences in the extent to which successive writers manifested a given complex of traits of whatever character. Similarly, the contrarieties basic to the history may range from contrasts between an initial non-existence of something and its eventual emergence fully formed (with its possible later disappearance) to clear-cut oppositions of characteristics of the same order with or without intermediate gradations between the first and the last. The

34

immediate moving causes, finally, are the productive acts of the writers involved in the change as these are conditioned, immediately or remotely, by the artistic or extra-artistic ends which the writers sought to realize in the process of construction, by the character of their literary, moral, and intellectual habits, and by the accidents of their social status, education, experience, and reading or of the events or circumstances which occasioned the writing of particular works.

It is evident that here again, as in organic literary history, we have moved beyond the simple principles of succession and of likeness and difference, though without ceasing to employ these as guides in the ordering and interpretation of data. The structure of a narrative history, like that of an organic history, is continuous and dynamic rather than atomistic and static, and its constituent elements, like those of an organic history, are related to one another as contraries or opposites. In both types of history, moreover, the problem of relevance is solved through the use of a previously determined system of concepts, and in both types there is an assumption of necessity.

At this point, however, the contrast begins, and philosophically considered, it is a fundamental one. In the first place, the continuity achieved in narrative history is the continuity not of a dialectical integration of historical differences in terms of a single analogy or scheme. Rather it is the continuity of a sequence of distinct events connected causally by whatever individual men or groups of men, through a period of time, happened to do with respect to the element constituting the continuum of the change. Accordingly, the degree of integration attainable in such a history depends upon the possibility of discovering causal connections, in materials, techniques, forms, or ends, among the different sequences with which it deals. The particular contrarieties in a narrative history, therefore, cannot be deduced from any unified scheme of common terms as, for example, in the dialectical histories of Taine and Cazamian. Inasmuch as their function is to signify initial, terminal, and intermediate points in a change, their selection (out of the store of possible significant differences in literary practice possessed by the historian) must always be a posteriori and relative to the specific matter of the change which is being traced. The concepts, furthermore, without

35

which the ordering of a narrative history and the determination of its criteria of relevance would be impossible are concepts of a very different sort from those on which the organic historian relies. What they represent is not a particular pattern of universals reflected in the history but simply a specification of the general causal factors which may be distinguished in any occurrence of change. They are not therefore constitutive concepts, determining the substance of the historian's elementary propositions, but heuristic concepts, determining the number and nature of the questions he must ask with respect to literary events about which he has already, and independently, made elementary propositions. And finally, although the construction of any coherent history entails the assertion of necessary connections among its happenings, the connections asserted in a narrative history are necessary not in any sense that implies determinism of a Marxist or psychological kind but only retrospectively, in the meaning of necessity involved in our saying, of something which has actually come about, that it could not have taken place as it did unless certain other things had happened previously.

That there have been many successful attempts to deal narratively with literary phenomena—taking these as events in particular sequences of change rather than as manifestations of more general principles and causes—hardly needs to be pointed out. Brief examples could be cited from many histories which, considered as wholes, are basically atomistic in structure (for example, Henry Hallam's *Introduction* and Douglas Bush's volume in the Oxford series), from a great number of scholarly articles and monographs, and from the writings of many literary critics (such as J. L. Lowes's *Convention and Revolt in Poetry* and several of Eliot's essays). The method has also been applied, on a larger scale, in the construction of literary biographies, of some of the better accounts of the origins and early development of drama and fiction, and of numerous studies in the history of genres, traditions of subject matter and technique, literary schools and movements, and the reputation and influence of writers. The characteristic virtues of the mode can be seen in such works—to mention only a few at random—as Alfred Jeanroy's *La Poésie lyrique des troubadours,* C. S. Lewis' *The Allegory of Love,* Ernest Bernbaum's *The Drama of Sensibility,* Paul Van Tieghem's *Ossian en France,* George Williamson's *The Senecan Amble,* and,

36

more comprehensive in scope than these, William Minto's *Literature of the Georgian Era* (a much neglected account of the changes in English poetry between Pope and Byron, interpreted in the context of other literary changes, which seems to me one of the least doctrinaire and most sophisticated books on its period I have read). Written with a minimum reliance on dialectical devices of historical construction, these histories, as well as a good many others like them, have the great merit, which is rarely encountered in the more ambitious histories, of telling, interestingly, complex and significant literary stories. Their limitations are chiefly the result of the kind of critical principles their writers have employed in discriminating the changing characteristics of works. For the most part, these historians have tended to rely either on grammatical or qualitative statements about the content and form of works or on inferences concerning the artistic intentions of writers of which the critical premises are at best definitions of techniques or generic differentiations of literary kinds. Their narratives, as a consequence, admirable as many of them are, have tended to stop short both of the fullest possible literary particularity and of the completest possible adequacy of historical explanation.

The next logical step, therefore, seems to be an extension and further refinement of narrative literary history on the basis of the one critical concept which is here left out, or utilized only inexplicitly and with respect only to its most general implications.

We have already said that in any history founded on the principle of artistic synthesis the central though by no means exclusive emphasis would be on the constructional aspects of literary works considered from the point of view of the problems faced by writers in the process of making poems, dramas, or narratives of different kinds. The collective enterprise of historians in this mode would consequently have as its ultimate purpose the writing of a narrative-causal history of the various literary arts in terms of four things: (1) the successive shifts in the artistic or formal ends which writers at different times and in different places have pursued, (2) the successive changes in the materials through which the different ends were realized, (3) the successive discoveries of more effective or at least new devices and techniques for the achievement of the different forms in the different materials, and

37

(4) the successive actualizations of all these changing possibilities in the production of artistically valuable or historically significant works in the different arts with which the history deals. For reasons we have noted, the relation between the first three of these elements—forms, materials, techniques—is such that they must be viewed, relatively to the preconstructional choices of writers, as independent variables; so it is possible to make any one of them by itself the organizing line of change in a history, as has often been done for materials and techniques in the partial mode of narrative history just discussed. It is the distinguishing assumption, however, of the kind of history we are now considering that complete historical intelligibility demands not only the inclusion of all three elements but the recognition that the first is necessarily prior in importance (though not always prior in the historian's order of inquiry) to the other two, since in the actual construction of literary works of a given kind the latter either depend upon it as a principle or are fully explicable, in all their peculiarities as combined in particular works, only by reference to it. It is appropriate therefore to describe this mode of literary history as the narrative history of forms.

The crucial problem, then, is the discrimination of the various artistic ends pursued by writers from time to time and the organization of these differences into significant lines of change. We need only recall here what has been said earlier about the first part of this task: it is not a question either of classifying works grammatically in terms of their conventional genres or of schematizing them dialectically in terms of a predetermined pattern of rational oppositions to which their differing characteristics are reduced; rather it is a question of distinguishing with adequate precision, in terms of the constructive principles operative in each, the generic and specific natures of the concrete wholes which writers, for one reason or another, chose to produce, and of doing this in such a fashion as clearly to indicate, for any group of works thus differentiated, the peculiar formal requirements which the choice of this principle rather than of some other, in the shaping of the material, imposed upon their writers. And the problem is solved, we may also recall, when the historian is able to say, for any work distinguished thus and so in medium and manner, that its principal part is an organization of such and such specific elements of action, character, thought, or emotion, accomplished in

38

such and such a way, and endowed consequently with the power of inducing in attentive and perceptive readers such and such a sequence of specific effects.

How seldom discriminations of this sort have been attempted in literary history can be easily illustrated. It is impossible to learn, for example, from any of the elaborate accounts we have of the serious English drama of the seventeenth century how many of the plays commonly called "tragedies" had plot forms of the highly particularized type analyzed by Aristotle in *Poetics* 13 and 14 (although we may suspect that apart from Shakespeare the number was small) and how many, on the contrary, owed their peculiar character to their authors' preference for various other formally distinct though allied ends. If then we are to trace with any precision or artistic intelligibility the history of English "tragedy" during this and subsequent periods down to the present, we need to have, as a starting point, far more adequate answers to this question than can be inferred from the existing histories, valuable as many of these are for their accounts of dramatic materials and conventions.

It is much the same with the histories of the English novel. Where can we discover, for example, how Fielding's novels are related, not materially and technically only but formally, to the fiction and drama that preceded him—or even to one another; or what were the formal innovations, if any, of Jane Austen; or to what different artistic forms Henry James adapted his various techniques of narrative and how far these forms were carried by him beyond the stage of differentiation they had already attained; or how the "modern" adventure stories of writers like Graham Greene differ in their formal principles, if they do, from the "classic" adventure fiction of R. L. Stevenson; or whether the historical significance of Ernest Hemingway is exhausted when we have finished discussing his contributions of fresh subject matter and new tricks of technique.

Nor is the case different when we turn to the histories of English poetry. Although much has been written about the changes in materials, attitudes, and dictional devices between Metaphysical poetry and Augustan, between Augustan and Romantic-Victorian, and between Victorian and "modern," can any one be justified in saying, on the basis of these discussions, that this is the whole of the story or that there were not likewise far-reaching shifts, in each of these periods,

39

in poetic forms, the consequences of which for the other aspects of the successive revolutions in poetry the historian ought also to consider? And even if, contrary to all probability, this was not the case—even if, during the whole period from 1600 to the present, no important new forms of lyric or didactic poetry emerged and no important new possibilities of further differentiation were discovered in the old ones—should we not at any rate be told precisely what the various forms were in relation to which, collectively or separately, the various material and technical changes took place?

It could well be that a concerted effort by many historians, equipped with sufficiently delicate tools of analysis, to give us the accurate discriminations among formal ends now so generally wanting would have the effect of renewing decisively our understanding of the course of English or any other literature in its various periods and branches. It would in any case serve to direct our attention more sharply than has yet been done to a major cause of both continuity and variability in literary practice. The history as finally constructed would not be exclusively a history of forms, although it would be this primarily in the sense that the historian's formal distinctions among works would serve to order narratively, as either lines of continuity or end terms of change, his propositions concerning the materials and technical operations in and by which the forms were achieved. Such a history would stop short of the kind of "integration" that presupposes, throughout or at any stage, a single analogy or a fixed and necessary scheme of development, but the historian of forms would be able to find partial substitutes for these devices, more in keeping with the a posteriori assumptions of his method, in certain theoretical considerations about the causal relationships of literary ends. Thus we may say that two distinguishable kinds of poetry are related subsumptively when the kind developed later implies as one of its necessary conditions of existence the previous development of the other kind, different though the two are in the specific nature of their organizing principles. We recognize, for example, that before writers can make unified structures having a sustained emotional power of a certain specific sort they must previously have learned how to achieve emotional interest and suspense of a less formal kind in the parts of works. It goes without saying that in the actual history of literature the movement is not always or everywhere from the more material to the more formal stages of such theoretically established relationships. It may be, for instance, that in a given historical situation, while writers of prose fiction are going from relatively general and diffuse emotional effects to more unified and particularized effects (as in the evolution of the "comic romance" between Scarron and Fielding), writers of tragedy are moving in the opposite direction (as in the history of tragic forms between Shakespeare and the later eighteenth century); or that shorter forms are at one time elaborated into larger (as in the relation of Richardson's first two novels to the earlier "pathetic" tales) and at another time longer forms as compressed into shorter (as in the relation of the full-length Gothic romances to the later short stories of Poe and others); or that, within a given species like tragedy, the development is at one stage characterized by the addition of new plot elements to those already in use to yield more complex emotional structures (as in the relation of Shakespeare to Kyd and Marlowe) and at another stage by the simplification and re-ordering of earlier plot forms in terms of one of their subordinate elements (as in the relation between Robert Dodsley's *Cleone* and *Othello*).

Employed as a heuristic device rather than as a constitutive principle, however, this notion of subsumptive relations among forms may be of the greatest utility to the historian in the analysis and ordering of his data. And it may be supplemented by similar general considerations bearing on the relative importance of different lines of formal change. From a historical point of view, the most significant shifts in literary ends are clearly those to which the historian can refer—as their necessary or probable consequences—the greatest number or variety of other changes in the kinds of materials writers chose to exploit and in the kinds of devices of construction, characterization, thought, imagery, diction, prosody, or representation they invented or revived for the purpose. Generally speaking, it may be assumed—again as not a dogma but a rough guide in interpretation—that a widespread shift on the part of the ablest writers from the cultivation of mimetic to the cultivation of didactic forms (such as occurred after the middle of the seventeenth century) is likely to have more far-reaching results of the kinds mentioned than a shift from serious forms to comic in drama or fiction, and that a shift of the latter sort is likely to be considerably more consequential than one involving only such formal

41

differences, significant though these are, as can be discerned between Shakespeare's earlier and later tragedies or between Congreve's *Double Dealer* and his other comedies or between *Pride and Prejudice* and *Emma* or *Persuasion*.

The problem of changes in literary ends can be treated apart from the problem of changes in literary materials, but only at the cost of rendering the statements about forms unhistorical and abstract; and conversely, although changes in materials can be, and repeatedly have been, made independent objects of study apart from forms, this has always been at the risk either of leaving the changes unexplained or of finding the explanation in causes which have only a remote bearing on the transformations necessarily effected in any body of materials when it is used as the matter of literary works. The historian of forms must therefore talk about changes in materials, but from the point of view not of the history of religion, culture, ideas, society, or language merely but of the history of the literary arts. Taking materials broadly, as comprising everything in the diction of a work or in the things signified by the diction—that is, story (as distinct from plot), environing circumstances, types or signs of character, objects or indexes of emotion, attitudes, conceptions, images, modes of argument, and the like—that can be referred to antecedents other than the writer's formal end and technical skill, whether the antecedents are in real life or in conventions of earlier literature, the historian will concern himself with these primarily as they have been formed for literary use either by particular efforts of previous artists or by the more general influence of past or contemporary ideas in attaching special significances and values to this or that aspect of experience. The most important changes will be those which necessitated or made probable the development of new formal effects or new technical devices on the part of the writers touched by them. Many instances of this could be given: the romances, lyrics, and allegories which in the twelfth century exploited the recently articulated doctrines of courtly love; the Renaissance dramas in which the plot materials of Greek romance suggested new effects; the rise of new formal varieties of comedy, tragedy, fiction, and poetry during the eighteenth century in response to the contemporary exaltation of "good nature"; the proliferation of new species of poetry, drama, and romance after 1750 as a consequence of the Medieval Revival; the emergence in our time of original plot forms in drama and novel in obvious adjustment to the fresh conceptions and values made current by Freud, and of new types of diction and rhythm in poetry and narrative in similar adjustment to modern linguistics and the general relaxation of verbal taboos. The historian of forms will avoid unduly schematizing such changes (as is done, for instance, in Stopford Brooke's account of changes in poetic subject matter between Shakespeare and Wordsworth and more completely still in Bateson's *English Poetry*). At the same time he will look beyond short-run and accidental differences to the broad lines of continuity that connect the successive major importations into artistic literature of new regions of physical, moral, and psychological experience: the successive shifts of interest, attitude, or knowledge which bring it about in a given age that certain themes or aspects of life formerly central in literary creation become incapable of stimulating any except the most old-fashioned writers or that situations and characters once thought appropriate only to comic forms are now exploited for serious effects, or vice versa; and the successive changes in literary opinion and practice with respect to the kinds of language or meter which are or are not proper, at different times, to literature or any of its kinds. In this consideration of such problems, finally, the historian will attempt to make clear the relation of particular material changes to contemporary changes in forms, discriminating between those changes in matter which affected simultaneously a number of important forms, those whose consequences were limited to one or two forms, and those which, emerging first in one form, were later, perhaps much later, extended to others.

The problem of changes in techniques is susceptible of generally similar treatment. The term techniques may be given a somewhat extended meaning, in this context, to signify any distinguishable modes of procedure which are the consequences, in a particular work, of its author's desire to impose on certain selected materials, invented by him or borrowed from earlier writers, a certain specific form or power, whether imitative or didactic; it includes thus a wide range of things, from the material organization of the plot or argument or lyric situation, the establishment of probable or necessary relations between its parts, the depiction of characters, and the elaboration of thought, down to the handling of diction, imagery, symbols, and verse and of all the devices of representation, literal or symbolic, which may be used to keep the minds of readers or spectators properly directed and to enhance, functionally or decoratively, the intended effect of the whole or of any of its parts. These are all things which writers can learn from other writers and then develop further in response to the material or formal exigencies of new works; they can therefore have a history of their own distinct from the histories of the materials and forms in relation to which they are used. Many parts of this history have indeed been written, so that the historian of forms has already available to him a considerable body of relevant data. He will need to review existing knowledge, however, in the light of his understanding of the varied artistic functions which the devices hitherto discussed—usually with exclusive reference to their material characteristics—may serve in works of different kinds. He will also need to supplement these observations with observations of his own. For example, there is nowhere in print, so far as I am aware, an adequate study of the many experiments in narrative manner which preceded Fielding and upon which he built. Again, despite all that has been written about the dramatic conventions of the early seventeenth century, I can think of no one who has inquired analytically into the extraordinary variety of choral devices (of action, character, thought, diction, and representation) which Shakespeare employed, especially in his tragedies, to affect the opinions and sympathies of his audience relative to the action in its successive parts. And similar gaps could be pointed out in other fields—most glaringly, perhaps, in the history of the modern lyric, where research has hardly gone beyond questions of versification and the grammatical or dialectical study of imagery.

In constructing a history of changes in techniques the historian of forms will attend to the particular artistic uses for which new devices of all kinds were invented; he will distinguish between the kind of invention that consists in adapting new devices to old formal uses and the kind that consists in finding new formal uses for old devices; he will dwell on the numerous efforts of writers to renew forms of poetry, drama, or fiction by borrowing devices from other forms, poetic or not (as eighteenth-century novelists, for example, obtained new effects by taking over devices from comedy, satire, and the essay), or by borrowing from the same or similar forms as cultivated in a more novel way in other literatures (as Eliot revivified English poetry by bringing into it techniques already developed in France); he will concern himself with the survivals of old devices in the face of belief by the more advanced or sensitive writers that their utility is exhausted; and he will call attention to the curious results that come about when, as often happens, a device appropriate and powerful in one species of poetry is adapted to uses it is incapable of serving effectively in another (as in the attempts of the Warton brothers to employ Miltonic blank verse in poems much closer in form to *Il Penseroso* than to *Paradise Lost*). He will not commit himself to an assumption of steady progress in the techniques any more than in the principles or forms of art, but he will be directed in his interpretations of successive technical differences by general considerations similar to those available to him for tracing changes in form. We may thus say theoretically, though with the proviso that in any given situation in history the order may be reversed, that there is a tendency in the literary arts to move from generality to particularity in the construction of plots (or their lyric equivalents) and in the definition and depiction of characters, from a concern with the immediate and external aspects of actions to a concentration on their internal aspects or their indirect consequences in the feelings of the agents or their friends, from simple and explicit indications of character, thought, or motive to elaborate and subtle indications, from highly articulated modes of speech to more elliptical and suggestive modes, from a fashion of imagery in which the reference is primarily to objects to one in which the inner state of the characters is more fully involved, from simple metaphors to complex and difficult ones, from verse having relatively few rhythmic dimensions to verse having many, from contentment with "statement" to insistence upon "rendering," from a minimum reliance on inference or indirect representation to a maximum reliance on these—and so on through many analogous probabilities of development by which the historian of forms may be guided, with due respect to the facts before him, in defining his lines of continuity and change.

The final problem of the historian in this mode arises from the obvious fact that the three elements so far considered, treated in abstraction from their synthesis in completed literary works, have the status only of possibilities, that is to say, of materials separated from the forms actually achieved by writers in constructing individual poems, plays, epics, or novels. The concrete realities and hence the distinctive characters of all the various arts reside in their products; it is to the successful making of these that the formal, material, and technical decisions of artists are directed, and it is of these, as made thus and so, that we predicate, in the first instance at least, significance or value. The historian of the literary arts must therefore find ways of dealing with the individual works within his field of interest that will do justice at once to their multiple historical relations and to their qualities as unique artistic wholes the production of which marked the coming into being of values, great or small, such as the world had not previously known.

Of the problem as stated in these terms no complete solution is possible in any of the other modes of literary history we have examined. For those historians who have been content with philological devices of analysis, the question of artistic value remains implicit, or rather is answered prior to the history itself in their decisions about what writers to include and what relative space to give to each; their characterizations of individual works, as we have seen, are restricted to grammatically distinguishable traits of "content" and "form"; and their judgments of historical significance dwell exclusively on such topics as the priority or originality or the typicality of particular works in relation to developments in materials and techniques and the extent of their popularity with readers or of their influence on subsequent production.

For those historians who have been concerned dialectically with general qualities of poetry or literature, these same devices are still available, but they are supplemented by others the general effect of which is to shift the locus of both literary value and historical significance from works to their writers, in terms of some variant of the ancient doctrine which made human discourse, of whatever kind, a reflection or "imitation" of the soul. In histories thus conceived, as we noted earlier, the emphasis may be either primarily "literary" or primarily "historical."

In the former case (well illustrated in Quintilian, Johnson's *Lives*, and the histories or historical essays of Hallam, Eliot, Leavis, and Cleanth Brooks) the values imputed to works are values which they possess by virtue of their authors' approximations to or departures from an ideal definition of literary or poetic excellence, statable in terms either of a dialectical composition of contrary general qualities or of a particular canon of writers who have most completely realized the ideal or, most commonly, of the two together. Much of the literary part of Hallam's history, thus, is an account of the triumphs, partial triumphs, and defeats of "good taste" or the "classical style" in poetry, drama, and literary prose; and the ruling concern of Leavis in his *Revaluation* is to discriminate between those poets and "lines" of poets who most adequately exemplify the proper adjustment of intelligence and emotion in poetry and those who depart from this norm in either of the two possible directions; his canonical writers include Shakespeare, Donne, Jonson, Pope (at times), Wordsworth (in certain respects), and Keats, and his remarks on individual poems turn consistently on their degree of participation, irrespective of their specific forms or ends, in what is thus constituted as the best "tradition."

When the primary emphasis of the historian is not literary in this sense but "historical," the two kinds of valuation tend to become identical (as notably in Taine and Leslie Stephen), and the relative greatness or importance of works is referred to the relative greatness or importance of their writers as men representing, more or less completely, major combinations or disjunctions of the psychological or social factors discriminated in the underlying dialectic. Occasionally, of course, the two extremes are combined, with the historian's judgment moving from the first level to the second, as when Eliot remarks that the "quality" he sees in Marvell is "probably a literary rather than a personal quality; or, more truly, . . . a quality of a civilization, of a traditional habit of life" or when Leavis discusses in similar fashion the "representativeness" of Jonson, Carew, Dryden, and Pope.

It is evident that in any of these histories, for all their radical differences, the judgments of literary value and historical significance are relative to either the preconstructional causes and conditions of works or to their postconstructional effects, seldom, and then only remotely, to the artistic ends of writers and the problems encountered by them in the actual process of making artistic syntheses of such and such kinds. The result is that individual works tend to lose their integrity as unique products of art and to appear in the history only as causes, consequences, instances, or signs of something else.

Now it would be foolish to assert that this is not an important part

47

of the truth about works, which the historian, if he aspires to give an adequate view of the literary past, must somehow bring into relief. And there is nothing in the assumptions underlying the narrative history of forms that makes it impossible for a historian of this school to formulate judgments which take this truth into account. His characterizations of works, as we have seen, can be made to include all the material discriminations possible in the philological method and at the same time general distinctions of quality derived, as in the dialectical method—but with a stricter attention to the literary causes of their manifestations in works—from the author's moral and intellectual personality and his relations to the culture and ideas of his time. He can deal likewise and as fully as historians of any other sort, with questions of material originality or conformity to tradition, with the effects of works on the writing of later works and on the taste and moral or doctrinal attitudes of readers, and with their representative character relatively to the literary practice or ideological currents of their age.

The important point, however, is that he is not restricted, in either his historical or his critical judgments, to a consideration of literary works merely in these somewhat general preconstructional and postconstructional terms. For, historically considered, individual works are not for him simply causes, consequences, or signs of other things. They are unique events in their own right: their significance cannot be adequately stated by treating their novelty as a function either of residual differences only (after the other traits of matter and manner have been assimilated to antecedent sources or traditions) or of any kind of dialectical division or recombination; rather it has to be exhibited, for any given work, in a narrative account of how its author solved the special problems of object, means, and manner set for him by his decision to give to his subject matter a certain specific artistic form and effect—in the course of achieving which he not only inevitably modified to some degree the traditional materials and techniques available to him but also revealed new possibilities in the form itself, perhaps even discovering a form as yet unattempted. In telling such a story the historian will necessarily adjust his statements to what he knows or can find out concerning the prior developments in forms, materials, and techniques employed by the work in question, but he will do this always with a view to the new state of affairs brought about by the work's appearance. He will make clear, thus, whether the consequences of writing it were to endow literature with an art form hitherto unknown, or with a masterpiece, having greater or less formal novelty, in a species already in process of development, or with a fresh variety of materials, or with new or more refined devices of technique of such and such kinds, or with some combination of these distinguishable types of value. The "placing" of any work in a history, and the character and proportions of the treatment accorded it, will depend upon what is thus revealed: of some works it will appear that their significance in these terms is multiple, of others that it is limited to one aspect alone; and although all works are events and no work is merely representative, the historian will often have to decide that the nature and magnitude of the novelty achieved by some works necessitates the fullest discussion of them as events, whereas others which innovated artistically in slighter degree can be introduced into his narrative, if they are introduced at all, merely as instances of what was generally being done. And the same work, of course, can appear as an instance of more than one thing.

The transition from such historical judgments of works to the consideration of their intrinsic and comparative literary values requires no change in the structure of the historian's narrative. For his first concern, we may repeat, is with the peculiar values which any literary work possesses by virtue of its writer's success in imposing on certain materials chosen by him for reasons of his own, a certain humanly interesting form, new or old, in such a manner as to enhance to the fullest extent the specific emotional or didactic force of which the form is capable. The intrinsic judgment of any work is therefore a judgment of its artistic success in the light of its distinctive end and of the writer's invention or selection of better or worse means, from among those relevant to his task, for its maximum realization. Such a judgment and its verification of course presupposes sensitivity to the peculiar effects of different work on the part of both the historian and his readers. It also presupposes analytical insight into what the general and special requirements of the form attempted are and into the comparative effectiveness of different ways of actualizing it in words. The judgment itself, however, is relative always to the specific nature of the task in hand and hence not dependent on any particular standard or canon of literary or poetic excellence determined

49

in advance and thereafter applied dialectically to all kinds of works. In addition, comparative judgments of two sorts are possible. The starting point of the first is again the experienced effects of the work, and the judgment consists in tracing these to their causes in the relative scope, maturity, or penetration of the ideas and moral attitudes presupposed by the construction of the work as a whole when it is compared with other works of the same or an earlier time. The starting point of the second is the peculiar difficulties which confronted the writer of a given work either because of the character of his materials in relation to his intended form or because of the state of development attained by the techniques of his art when he wrote, and the judgment consists in pointing to the traits of his achievement which it possesses in spite of or by reason of these. It can easily be seen that for the indication of any of these three kinds of judgments in a history no interruption of the causal sequence is required—no systematic intrusions, as in many histories, of summarizing paragraphs of praise or blame—but only such a shaping of the narrative statements about works, both those treated singly in detail and those treated collectively, as will allow the various reasons of success or failure, of development or decline, in the author's choices to appear. And the values so revealed will have a historical status inasmuch as they are the values that have emerged successively, and always in a clothing of historically determined conventions and accidents of material, in the actual course of development of the various literary arts. But at the same time, inasmuch as their realization involves the universal elements and principles contained in these arts, they will also appear as values of an absolute sort, in the sense that, once embodied in works, they can never again be resolved completely into the history from which they came.

These, then—forms, materials, techniques, and individual achievements—are the major variables which must be combined somehow in any adequate narrative history of literary forms. The possibilities of combination are many, but what these are and to what extent they permit the writing of unified histories dealing with many species of works, we shall be better able to see after we have inquired into the kinds of causal efficacy which, in this mode of history as contrasted with the other modes, may be assumed to bind literary events and changes together and to connect them with other things.

3. Principles of Explanation

The contrast is sharpest, as one might expect, with the conception of causality found in histories of the organic type. The possibility of constructing a history of this sort depends, in the first place, upon the assumption that the "real" as distinguished from the "apparent" or "superficial" causes of what writers do are to be found in a single factor or complex of factors present throughout the particular history, or in history generally, to which all the more specific or local factors can be related as consequences or manifestations. Explicit statements of the assumption frequently occur, especially in those historians, like Taine and Cazamian (to say nothing of the Marxists), who exemplify its implications most consistently. "Comprendre," writes Cazamian, "c'est unifier"; and he illustrates his maxim in a sketch of English literature between 1660 and 1914 in which each phase of the development is treated as the necessary product of two factors, one internal, the other external: "l'évolution psychologique d'une part, la pression du milieu historique et social de l'autre." The problem of the historian at each successive point, he remarks, is to examine the joint effect of these two forces. Not all integrating historians have been as systematic in their search for unitary explanation, but the taste for it has been constant in this tradition and has infected also the thinking of a good many critics and scholars who would undoubtedly repudiate the notion of causal monism if it were put to them in so many words.

The tendency has taken many forms. It can be seen in the disposition of innumerable historians to prefer one type of causality to all other possible types—to insist, for example, that diction is the most important element in poetry and that consequently differences between particular poets and general changes in poetry are determined primarily by differences or changes in "the attitude to language"; or that the fundamental determinants are alterations in subject matter; or that they are to be looked for in the relations of authors to their contemporary audience; or that the only real explanation is a psychoanalytical one; or that the operation of causes runs always in a single direction (for example, from having something to say to finding a suitable form in which to say it); and so on. The tendency can be seen also in the common belief that the history of literature is always most intelligible when it is correlated with some one other line of develop-

51

ment, this being identified variously by different historians—sometimes as the history of religion, sometimes as the history of culture in the anthropological sense, sometimes as the history of philosophic or popular ideas, sometimes as the history of the class struggle or of some other socio-economic classification of phenomena. And these presuppositions have usually gone along with the conviction that each age or period distinguished in literary history possesses a characteristic unity of "spirit" from the statement of which (however radically different this may be in different histories) consequences follow as to what writers did, or even had to do.

Whatever the unifying cause or hierarchy of causes in any particular history of this type, it is obvious—as a second trait of the method —that the relation of such a cause to the concrete effects in literary works it is designed to explain can be only that of a more or less remote antecedent. The quest is typically, indeed, for "underlying" causes, such as the national character, the temper or "sensibility" of the age, the broad movement of society or of collective thought, the dominant spirit of the ruling class, the particular "moment" of a profound psychological evolution, the prevalence of a certain all-inclusive Weltanschauung, the "general conditions of culture and civilization"—for causes, that is, which do not affect writers immediately as artists of a certain kind struggling with the problems of individual literary works but more remotely as men belonging to large groups, classes, or generations of men all but a few of whom are not artists at all. Authors of such histories rarely introduce any mediating causal steps between the integrating principle and the peculiarities of content and form exhibited by the works it purports to explain. The result is that we are never given the sufficient causes of literary works considered as concrete objects or events (if we are given causes at all) but only the conditions *sine qua non* of the presence in some works and the absence from others of certain combinations of general traits. It is as if, seeking to explain the fact that I sometimes make good fires in my fireplace and sometimes poor ones, I should take into account only the shape and size of the chimney and the economic origins of the logs.

The reasoning used to connect causes and effects, moreover—and this is a third trait of the method—seems to proceed normally from general antecedent conditions, as better known, to particular observable characteristics of writers and works, as relatively more obscure, that is, forward from the cause or principle, as in mathematics, rather than backward to it, as in ordinary history or in our attempts to diagnose practical situations in common life. It is thus habitual among these historians to speak of authors and literary styles or movements as being "produced" by their "age" or by the social or cultural "conditions" amid which they flourished. This kind of language has become so common that it takes a second or third reading to see anything curious in a statement like the assertion, in a recent essay, that the "limited sense of continuity" said to be characteristic of the eighteenth-century world view "led Pope and Johnson to prefer certain sorts of literature to others," namely, to neglect narrative and connected argument, although it is conceded that these forms were being cultivated by many writers during the same time.

Such statements are indeed curious if they are taken in the literal sense suggested by their words. For their validity as causal propositions is then made to depend upon the illicit assumption that we can deduce particularized actuality from general possibility, the emergence of completed forms from the prior existence of their elements. It is reasonable to suspect, however, in view of the widespread use by intelligent historians of this mode of inference, that we are wrong in thinking it to be literal causal inference at all. The truth is, as we recognize increasingly the more we examine the histories in which such propositions occur, that most of their writers are not primarily interested in individual literary works for their own sake but in these chiefly as signs of deeper or larger realities and that what we tend to interpret as causal explanations are not really assertions of causal efficacy in any literal sense but rather quasi-Platonic statements of a quite different sort, resting on assumptions in which we may discern, for all the intrusions of literal or "Aristotelian" language, the notions of the divided line and of the participation of the Many in the being of the One.

It is this philosophic bias rather than methodological incompetence, we must suppose, that has led the better historians of the organic school to concentrate on the discovery of single "causes," to seek these by preference in factors remote from the constructed particularity of works, and to argue the connections of "causes" and "effects" in a seemingly a priori way. The result in the more elaborate histories is an interpretative dialectic that moves in two stages, the first of which is a simple application of the principle of the divided line, the second of which involves also the idea of participation. The consequences of the first assumption we have already noted—in the universal tendency of these histories to treat the characteristics of literary works as "reflections" or "symbols" of the (comparatively more "real") traits of their authors and, through these, taken again as "images" or "expressions," of the society or state of civilization or age which "produced" them, through a hierarchy of imitation-object relations the final term of which is the unifying reality of the history. The consequences of the second assumption are seen most clearly, perhaps, in the extreme developments of the organic method which have distinguished the German tradition of *Geistesgeschichte*. Here the interpretative relationships run horizontally, so to speak, from particular masses of phenomena to other particular masses in terms of likeness or analogy, the unifying "causal" reality being the dialectical whole which, whether it is explicitly named or not, is constituted by the pattern of these relations between its parts. The device, pushed to the limits of metaphorical daring through the discovery of what Spengler called "deep uniformities" among the most disparate historical phenomena, is exemplified to the point of parody in Paul Meissner's *Die geistesgeschichtlichen Grundlagen des englischen Literaturbarocks*. Employed somewhat more modestly to bind together concurrent qualities or changes within limited fields of generic difference, it is to be met with nowadays in the writings of nearly all critics and historians whose starting point is a conviction of the interrelatedness of the arts with one another and of any or all of these with the general movement of society or thought in any age; for instance, in the reproach directed against a recent critic of Matisse for not perceiving the significance of "that great change from three to two-dimensionality which modern art has effected in pictorial space—a change that expresses our industrial society's abandonment of Cartesian rationality for empiricism and positivism"; or in the insistence by a more sober historian of the American mind that "no one who studies the career of Ezra Pound can doubt that the search for obscurity was related to hatred of democracy." That a lurking presumption of causal efficacy underlies, or can easily be read into, statements like the last is of course obvious; the point is that the historian who

54

makes such assertions in an organic history is under no obligation to render this explicit or to argue its plausibility for the relationship in question or even to commit himself to saying that of two terms thus related one represents cause and the other effect. It is true that in relationships in which one term is literary and the other social, political, psychological, or ideological, the second is usually assumed to be more fundamental, but this means, at least in the stricter applications of the method, being either closer to the nature of the complex which is being constituted or else better known. It is enough if two or more things can be brought together by analogy in such a way as to make them parts of a common whole, small or large, the qualities of which, as signified by their likeness, they all share (though some or one of them more fully or obviously than the others).

This is a perfectly legitimate method of interpreting the literary past, capable of giving us, in the hands of philosophically minded and trained historians (like Leslie Stephen, for example), illuminating insights not easily arrived at by any other way. The typical corruptions of the method are two: on the one hand, irresponsible analogizing, uncontrolled by any dialectically rigorous criticism of terms and hence often debased to the level of mere verbal equivocation, as constantly in Spengler, Meissner, and other extreme devotees of *Geistesgeschichte;* and on the other hand, overliteralization, uncontrolled by any clear understanding of the ideals and limits of the procedure and hence frequently leading to statements of equations, correspondences, and identities among disparate phenomena which are hard to distinguish from bad or unverifiable propositions of cause and effect; as, for example, in the sentence about Ezra Pound—we can hardly help asking, apropos of this, whether there is indeed any necessary or probable relation between "obscurity" in poetry and "hatred of democracy" such as would justify, in any concrete instance, making the latter in a literal sense the cause of the former.

There are many traces of this kind of ambiguity in recent works, especially British and American, in which historians trained in critical or philological techniques—and hence more respectful of texts than their German contemporaries—have attempted to relate literature, in various particular ways, to the evolution of society and ideas. It can be detected in Douglas Bush's interpretation of early seventeenth-century literature in the light of the conflict between the

55

Christian-Humanist tradition and the new materialism, where, although writers and literary schools are consistently treated as "parts" and "signs" of "larger" movements, there is at the same time a considerable admixture of the literally causal; in F. R. Leavis' correlations of poets, in his *Revaluation,* with changes in "civilization," where it is often hard to know whether we are being given highly suggestive analogies or merely amateurish social history; and in René Wellek's papers on the unity of Romanticism, where our appreciation of the synthesizing insights is often thwarted by a sense of the literal differences in form or method among particular writings which his system of equations does not wholly conceal. Lastly, and in a rather striking way, the same ambiguity is seen in the series of books by Hardin Craig, Theodore Spencer, E. M. W. Tillyard, and others, on the relations between Shakespeare and the Elizabethan "world picture," where a dialectically constructed scheme of ideas, pieced out from many texts, among which passages in Shakespeare are of key importance, is first predicated of the age as a whole and then used as a principle in the explanation of the plays: we are tempted to cry out against the circularity of this until we realize that despite these authors' frequent assimilation of their method to that of ordinary philological history they are not dealing really in causal sequences of events but only in relationships of participation among phenomena joined by analogy.

Whatever compromises or confusions may be exhibited by particular historians of this school, their basic procedures in effecting links between the elements of their histories remain clearly distinct, as founded on quite different aims and philosophic assumptions, from those of the narrative historian of literary forms. The historian of forms cannot indeed dispense with analogies, but he will use these not as principles of interpretation but as heuristic devices in the discovery of dynamic connections among facts which it will then be his business to try to explain in literal terms. For his task, unlike that of the organic historian, is not to clarify literary particulars by treating them as "parts" of more easily apprehended wholes. Rather it is to preserve the integrity of particular literary achievements while making them intelligible historically in terms (a) of the individual acts that resulted in their production and (b) of the context of continuous changes in literary forms, materials, and techniques to which these acts were related as effects or causes. He is therefore compelled to seek for causes in the ordinary sense of the word: causes, in the first instance, of what particular writers did in solving the problems presented by particular works and, beyond or behind these, causes of the various collective changes with respect to which the works were events. The only ultimate realities he will be concerned with are literary works conceived of as concrete wholes possessing distinctive powers by virtue of the peculiar manner in which their diverse elements were selected, treated, and combined. He must attempt both to trace the separable elements to their origins and to account for their treatment and combination, and this with reference always to observable differences in the principles of construction upon which the final result depended in different works.

He cannot assume, accordingly, that the causes he is looking for will always be of the same kind or operate in the same order of priority or exert the same relative degree of compulsion, or that they can ever be resolved into or deduced from any single "underlying" cause valid for the whole history. He will not of course suppose that there are no causal interrelations among the happenings or developments he assigns as the causes of particular acts or that he can never uncover "general causes" linking many different kinds of works with one another or with contemporary changes in society, politics, and thought. But he will treat these remoter causes as secondary to the proximate or immediate causes which account for the specific literary phenomena he is primarily concerned to explain, and he will not insist on them unless he can indicate at least a plausible series of intermediate causes connecting them with their assumed literary effects.

He will distinguish, however, between the necessary conditions of an event or change, in the sense of those antecedents without the occurrence of which we cannot imagine how it could have taken place (as we may say, for example, that the development of dramatic blank verse by Marlowe was a necessary condition of Shakespeare's achievement in writing dialogue) and the sufficient conditions, in the sense of the convergence of proximate material, final, and efficient causes upon which its actual occurrence as an event or change of such and such a character can be shown to have depended in a positive way;

57

and he will always seek, as far as his data permit, to move from the former to the latter.

His procedure will differ, finally, from that of the organic historian (or what often seems to be the procedure in organic histories) in being analytical rather than synthetic—in treating causal statements, that is to say, as a posteriori hypotheses made necessary or plausible by the peculiar character and combination of the elements discernible in a given work or group of works. These he will always take as better known and reason back from them to what had to happen or exist, including accidents as well as purposeful actions, before they could have become what they evidently are. He will argue, thus, from completed works to the specific artistic ends and problems they presuppose; from the ends and problems to the reasoning implicit in the particular choices and combinations of means affected by writers in relation to them; from the means as used to the antecedent events and circumstances implied by the writers' preference for these means over others as well or better suited, theoretically, to their ends; and from the ends as chosen to the previous happenings, in the minds of the writers and in the general situation, necessitated hypothetically by their choice.

It follows from these three differences that the causal explanations offered by the historian of forms will have much in common with, and will indeed subsume while supplementing and reordering, the kinds of explanation commonly found in literary histories based on a philological approach to texts. The causes asserted in these histories have normally been of two sorts: (a) those which relate the elements of subject matter and technique combined in particular works to their sources in earlier literature or in the life and thought of the time; and (b) those which relate those elements to requirements or opportunities imposed by the tastes or demands of audiences, critics, publishers, censors, stage managers, and the like (even when these are resisted), by the character of the special occasions which inspired particular works, and by the nature of the writers' constructive tasks as defined conventionally in the accepted rules and customs of the genres being cultivated (whether these are complied with or reacted against). I shall return later to the uses which the narrative historian of forms can make of both these types of causes; it is sufficient here to point out the limitations inherent in this mode of "literary history" or "historical criticism" when it constitutes the only resource of the historian or is made dogmatically exclusive of other principles of explanation. It is true enough, as one enthusiast for the method has insisted, that Shakespeare—or any writer—"must be reckoned a man among men, a man who can be understood only against the background of his own time," but surely the converse of this truth, which has been a commonplace since antiquity, is the further truth that any explanation which considers a work only against the background of the writer's own time, without taking account also of the specific nature of his art, is bound to be incomplete as historical understanding. We can know, for example, by philological means, that Shakespeare took the story of *Othello* from a novella by Cinthio and made certain changes in the sequence of events there set forth; but not why, in writing his play, he went to the trouble, for instance, of altering so drastically the events after the murder. So too, thanks to one of the triumphs of modern philology, we can trace a great proportion of the words in *Kubla Khan* to certain miscellaneous books of travel; but the delicate method by which these facts are established does not enable J. L. Lowes to make clear, except in terms of a myth about the creative imagination, why it was that only these few words, out of the hundreds of thousands which Coleridge must have read in the same sources, became part of the poem. And again, although Shakespeare, as we have been told so often, was doubtless a man of the theater, ambitious for immediate success in competition with his older and younger contemporaries, to argue from this cause alone to what he did in his tragedies is patently to make intelligible only the not very significant respects in which, in these plays, he relied on established conventions of plot, character, diction, and stage technique. It is to leave unexplained not only the peculiar uses he made of the conventions but the highly important fact that the tragedies he wrote were essentially different in kind, no less than in degree of excellence, from those of any of his rivals.

It is a natural tendency of scholars trained in this presumably "objective" method to assume that the questions it makes possible are the only questions concerning the causes of literary effects that can ever be properly answered or indeed require to be asked. An example among many others of this methodological dogmatism is a note by G. L. Kittredge on the curiously unhistorical character of Caesar in Shakespeare's play. "Was the historical Caesar," he asks, "so antipathetic to Shakespeare that he either could not or would not portray him adequately?" To answer the question, he says, is not difficult. "Caesar's lordly style, his pompous habit of speaking of himself in the third person has been adequately explained by reference to the Latin tragedy, *Julius Caesar*, by Muretus, first published in 1553. Muretus invested Caesar with the style and manner of Seneca's braggart Hercules, and this device had established a fashion: the audience expected the Caesarian dialect." That this is part of the story, and hence needs to be considered by any historian who aspires to causal sufficiency in his narrative, probably no one will question, but can we ever safely assert that any such important fact as the characterization of a key figure in a play by a first-rate dramatist is "adequately explained" until we have asked ourselves whether or not the peculiar plot form of the play could have been preserved had the characterization been of another sort—that is, had Shakespeare represented Caesar as other than "lordly" and "pompous"?

The conception of causality underlying the narrative history of forms would make provision for precisely such questions as this as well as for all the other types of causal problems now considered by philologists and literary historians which can be solved in literal terms.

We have seen why in a history of this kind there can be no unified structure or hierarchy of causes and effects. This does not mean, however, that the historian cannot attempt a general analysis of possible sources of novelty or change in literature which would serve him as a guide in his inquiries by suggesting, if not fixed relations of priority or dependence among causes themselves, at least a rough logical order in the questions he may ask concerning them. The basis of the order is given by the primary assumption upon which this mode of history depends, namely, that the values achieved in literature at any given time and the changes occurring with respect to these are what they are by virtue, immediately, of decisions made by individual artists in the process of thinking out and composing individual works and, more remotely, of antecedent conditions, influences, accidents, and so on which helped shape their purposes and habits as both artists and men. Of these two levels of causation—

60

constructional and preconstructional, proximate and more or less remote—neither can be neglected, but it is clear that though the first presupposes the second as its necessary substrate, it cannot be deduced from or resolved into it. It is also clear that we cannot know what causes of the second kind were operative in a given literary event or sequence of change until we have analyzed the more immediate causes in terms of which these become historically relevant.

The logically first inquiry of the historian is therefore into the constructional causes of the literary happenings he has to deal with. These may be divided into three groups, the first depending primarily on the nature of the specific art form which is being attempted, the second primarily on extraformal motives, incidental to this, in the writer himself, the third on the material circumstances of his productive acts.

Although critics and historians have hitherto made little of the fact, it cannot be doubted that once a competent writer has determined in a general way the material subject and scope of a work, as well as the general traits of its medium and manner, and has come to know, more or less clearly, what specific form, or emotional or didactic effect, he wants the completed work to produce, he must then begin to feel a certain objective compulsion, as to what he can or ought to do in the different parts of his work, that stems from the peculiar nature of the artistic task he has set for himself. There is plenty of testimony to this fact from writers who, like James in his *Notebooks,* have spoken in detail of their constructional problems, and it can be verified by any one who will recall the various necessities, not of his own making, he has had to face in writing anything, even an essay like this. Given a particular matter and a formal end of a particular sort, whether often successfully accomplished in earlier works or now for the first time discovered, it follows necessarily that some devices of plot (or other structure), character, thought, diction, or representation will be impossible for the writer to use, other devices indispensable, and still others advantageous in a lesser or greater degree if the form in view is to be realized with some approximation to its maximum power; and a writer becomes an artist when he knows, instinctively or upon re-

61

flection, why these things are so, and is able to embody his knowledge appropriately in what he writes.

For the historian these reasons, connecting the particular decisions of a writer in handling the parts of a given work with the requirements of a whole he is aiming to achieve, constitute what I shall call artistic or poetic causes; their operation resembles that of reasons of state, which, diverse as these are, tend to lead to strikingly similar choices when similar situations present themselves at any time no matter what the idiosyncrasies or ideologies of the statesmen concerned. And just as reasons of state are not always equally determinative, so the efficacy of artistic causes varies greatly from work to work or even in the production of a single writer specializing in a single form. We call those works masterpieces in the writing of which such causes appear to have operated with maximum compulsory force in the author's conception and treatment of all the parts both in themselves and with respect to their functions in sustaining and enhancing the effect of the whole. Such among no large number of others are *Hamlet* and *The Brothers Karamazov*. The historian will distinguish between the few works of this class that have ever been written and the many works in which, although an overall effect is achieved, some of the parts have been neglected, or in which, although all or some of the parts, such as diction, thought, and character, are highly developed, the whole remains comparatively unaffecting or obscure; and between these and those others, still more numerous, in which causes having little to do with art in any serious sense have tended to predominate.

We may divide reasons of art into two classes: those which pertain to conditions of success in writing common to all or to a number of literary forms and those which pertain characteristically to one or another specific form. For each of these the problem of the historian is double—to specify clearly the locus of the trait he is attempting to explain (as a trait of object, manner, or means) and to conjecture the principle or, as usually in the better works, combination of principles which makes intelligible, when this is not obvious or when the reason is not patently extra-artistic, what the writer has done.

The better known principles, and hence those most commonly invoked in the literary histories which do not eschew artistic explanations altogether, are naturally those operative in all or many distinct species of works. Explanations are relatively easy when we are dealing with skills generally desirable in all or in most works: methods of achieving clarity in diction or its avoidance, or of stating something economically or diffusely or leaving it to inference; of writing lively or stately dialogue, of rendering unspoken thought, of making characters or circumstances vivid, of giving probability to a sequence of acts, of effecting suspense or surprise; or generally of evoking or enhancing a particular emotion; or of deciding between a dramatic and a narrative manner, or a special variety of dramatic manner; or of choosing verse of one sort or another rather than prose.

Some of the causal discussions in the *Poetics* relate to effects of these general kinds, as in the connections indicated between Sophocles' introduction of a third actor and his desire for greater magnitude in his plots or between Homer's avoidance of speech in his own person and the conditions of imitation in narrative poems; a modern instance is T. S. Eliot's deduction of the differences between the actions and characters in Seneca's plays and those in Greek drama from the necessary limitations of plays written to be declaimed.

In artistically successful works, however, the operation of these general causes is bound to be controlled, to a greater or lesser extent, by causes arising from the specific requirements of the form relative to the matter being shaped by it. In such works, therefore, the historian's primary concern will be with these causes.

What, for example, would be the first interest of the historian of forms in dealing with a play like *Cymbeline?* Starting with the concrete plot as experienced and with a definition of the peculiar pleasure the play in fact yields, he would attempt to reconstruct the artistic reasoning which in effect, if not consciously at all points, guided Shakespeare's decisions as to what combination of what kinds of incidents linked by what kinds of probability this form demanded; how these ought to be developed, ordered, emphasized, or toned down in the dramatic representation; who the protagonist ought to be and what other character roles were necessary or desirable; what moral traits or mixtures of traits the dramatis personae ought to have and by what kinds of devices their respective qualities and thoughts could be best rendered and in what degrees of particularity; what varieties of suspense in the various parts should be aimed at and what avoided; how (since the form was to be that of a reconciliation tragicomedy) long-run confidence in the eventual reunion of the heroine and her husband could be sustained without lessening unduly the interest of the short-run expectation of evil and for this purpose what kinds of choral devices would be most effective; and what, finally, for any of the scenes or speeches, ought to be the structure and tone of the diction. Before Shakespeare could write *Cymbeline* as we have it, he had to solve all these as well as many subsidiary problems, and his achievement becomes intelligible as a literary event in proportion to the historian's success in linking the solutions Shakespeare hit upon with the final and intermediate formal ends they served in the play. And this link is discovered by means of general premises applicable to all works in which the ends and problems are the same. The middle terms in such causal arguments will be the "rules," specific to the different forms of literary art, which, as Pope said, are discovered not devised. They are thus distinct, as principles, from conventions and traditions, although they may be obscured, for poets as well as for critics, by the particular historical conventions poets have necessarily used in applying them, and although they tend to be forgotten easily, except as embodied in the traditions of the various poetic kinds effective on poets at a given time.

The history of the poetic arts considered as arts is the history of the gradual discovery by poets of such principles for one new literary form after another—for "punitive tragedy" after tragedy as Aristotle defined it, for the imitative lyric after the panegyrical ode, for the lyric of character or of "metaphysical" thought after the simple lyric of feeling, for sympathetic narrative comedy of the *Tom Jones* type after the dramatic satirical comedy of the ancients and Jonson, and so on. It is the history also of the refinement of such principles and their extension to new materials, of the invention of new techniques for their more effective operation in new subject matters or on the sensibilities of poets and readers weary of the older techniques, of their partial or complete neglect (as notoriously in English tragedy after the seventeenth century), of their rediscovery for particular forms (as for the various dramatic forms in the Renaissance and notably for the tragedy of pity and fear by Shakespeare), and so on in a complicated and often accidentally determined sequence which can end only when the desire to create new works of art disappears from mankind.

The first interpretative task of the historian of forms will thus be the recovery, for the works constituting the major events of his narrative, of the various reasons of art which presided in their making; in this he will rely on such theoretical studies of literary forms as are available to him, supplemented by his own insights into the psychological preconditions of particular literary effects. And he will also be able to generalize in these terms about the artistic causes operative collectively in large or small groups of works having in common the same formal end. It was noted by Aristotle, for example, that Greek writers of tragedy had tended to retain the historical names and many of the historical circumstances of the stories underlying their plots, and he found the reason for this in the fact that the tragic effect requires a high degree of probability in the incidents through which it is to be produced and in the further fact that we tend to take for granted the complete probability of anything we believe has actually occurred. This line of reasoning clearly makes sense out of their procedure, if we assume that the writers who established the tradition of historical subjects knew what they were about. And the artistic reason is logically prior, if it is really operative, no matter what extra-artistic reasons may be supposed to have contributed to the use of historical names, and no matter what alternative devices might have been used instead.

It is the same with many other equally general literary phenomena which are usually either left unexplained in histories or explained merely as instances of prevailing conventions or of the ineptitude of writers. A case in point is the tendency exhibited by most of the Gothic novelists of the eighteenth and early nineteenth centuries to endow their principal agents, whether heroes, heroines, or villains, with relatively little character and to represent them acting from simple, uncomplicated motives easily intelligible in the light of the situations they face. This doubtless detracts from the interest such works can have for serious minds, but the historian, before passing judgment, will ask whether the neglect of specificity and roundedness of character in the Gothic stories may not have been dictated, in some sense, by the artistic end their authors had in view, namely, a concentration on the mysteriously terrifying quality of

65

the events portrayed. To portray character in more vivid detail would either introduce moral issues conducive to something like tragic pity and fear or divert the reader's attention from the unusual and sinister happenings to the persons involved in them. What the form demanded, in short, was enough character to impel readers to take sides with some of the agents against others, as a result of natural sympathy, and nothing more; and that being precisely what the writers of these works tended to give, their practice becomes to the same extent understandable as a fact in literary history.

There is finally—if another example is needed—the famous problem of obscurity in contemporary poetry. The historian of forms will have little patience with large analogical explanations of this in moral or sociological terms until he has satisfied himself that the "obscurity" of at least the better poems is not made sufficiently intelligible by treating it as the consequence, partly indeed of their authors' desire to go beyond the relatively easy and explicit techniques of their immediate predecessors, but primarily of their interest in representing poetically complex and evanescent states of emotion and trains of associative or subconscious thought.

The intelligibility in all these cases depends on the possibility of reconstructing the artistic reasons of poets, novelists, and dramatists relatively to concrete poetic tasks, that is to say, of deducing what any such writer did with the *données* of a given work from the peculiar nature and requirements of its professed overall form insofar as this can be identified by the historian. That this can be done with illuminating results for many species of works even in the present state of our theoretical knowledge, I think there can be little question; the doing of it is indeed the distinguishing contribution of the narrative history of forms to the inquiry concerning the causes of literary events.

The clearer the historian is about the artistic causes of works, moreover, the better equipped he will be to assess properly the remaining factors in poetic production, those which stem from other causes besides the pure and impersonal desire to realize adequately a known poetic form or to experiment with new formal possibilities. It has been one of the limitations of contemporary criticism that its emphasis has been placed almost exclusively on these other ends—as in the current tendency to collapse the formal intentions of Shakespeare and Jane Austen, for example, into the "profound" moral convictions which were undoubtedly also effective in shaping the peculiar artistic character of their several works. The historian of forms will keep the two types of causation analytically distinct, but, on the other hand, he will give due weight—never quite the same perhaps for any two works even of the same author—to those traits of the works he discusses for which an explanation in terms of the form is either insufficient or irrelevant.

The distinction between poetic and other causes is most difficult in those works which most fully realize the potentialities of their respective kinds. We cannot doubt, on the one hand, even in the absence of external testimony, that works like *King Lear, Tom Jones,* and *Emma* would not be what they are except for their authors' preoccupation with significant moral issues. But so complete is the subsumption, in these and other masterpieces, of the moral by the poetic that in the historian's causal analysis the status of the former element, important as it is, necessarily becomes one of means rather than end. Masterpieces are exceptions, however, and the historian must also deal with a great many works the construction of which has obviously been influenced by competing aims, formal and extra-formal, with consequences ranging from incidental intrusions of matter difficult to explain on formal grounds to a more or less complete wrecking of the form. Between these extremes lie many works in which, as in Fletcher's tragicomedies, a concern with enhancing the separate effectiveness of parts leads to a general relaxation of the whole; many others in which, as in Dickens' *Hard Times* and perhaps Orwell's *1984,* the author's practical zeal, though quite compatible with the production of a fine didactic or imitative structure, is satisfied with immediately strong effects on a narrow audience through the use of frequently inferior means; and still others in which, as in *Don Quixote* and *Joseph Andrews,* although it is possible to discriminate two distinct ends, the extraformal end is not only kept subordinate to the other but, for the most part, made to serve simultaneously its peculiar needs. Works of the third kind present special problems of causal interpretation, the solution of which requires of the historian both a precise awareness of what the competing ends and their constructional consequences are and an analysis of their effects which will relate these clearly to the various elements of the work. To do justice to them, the critic must distrust facile explanations at the expense of the author, deriving from the oversimple assumption that any particular trait or device in a work must be accounted for by a single cause. The ends which compete with the specific dictates of the poetic form need not be extraliterary, however. The realization of a certain form in a certain matter may still be the controlling aim, but the choice of means for its realization may be determined in part at least (as in the composition of the *Lyrical Ballads*) by a desire to test or exemplify a new theory of poetic subject matter and language, or again (as in *Samson Agonistes*, Pope's *Imitations of Horace*, and Fielding's *Amelia*), by admiration for a particular model or tradition of writing and a desire to utilize its devices in giving form to new or different materials.

There are, lastly, many works belonging in neither of these two classes about which it would be futile for the historian to attempt to deduce much of what was done in the parts from the nature of the form—for the simple reason that the form was not the controlling end pursued by their writers. Their primary interest, that is to say, was not in achieving finished and moving works of imitative or didactic art but in exploiting, apropos of some more or less emotionally indifferent subject, the resources of a particular type of medium or technique either newly discovered by them or recently come into vogue. Their writers fall into two easily distinguishable groups: those in whom the technical or dictional interest is genuinely experimental (for example Ezra Pound, some of whose early poems, though historically of great importance, have the limited significance as poetic art of what A. R. Orage liked to call "studio work") and those in whom the same interest is predominantly ritualistic (as many of the technically minded minor poets who have written since Pound, Eliot, or Auden).

The historian of forms will take account of all such competing, supplementary, or partial ends in his interpretations of literary events; and he will not overlook, in the second place, the various material compulsions and accidents to which writers are subject, in differing degrees, while engaged in constructing works. A writer has always, for one thing, a contemporary audience in view, the specific character of which is bound to influence to some extent, often without full awareness on his part, the invention and handling of his matter—his choices among possible kinds of incidents and circumstances, his preferences for particular types of character and of signs for rendering these, his use of certain maxims and topics of argument or commentary rather than others, his selection of imagery, diction, and verse, and his decisions, frequently, as to what has to be made explicit and as to what can or should be left unsaid. Every work, no matter how perfect its art, inevitably reflects its audience in these and other similar ways through the moral, social, psychological, and literary conventions it employs. Less distinguished works do this more completely and obviously than the better ones; indeed, the least distinguished works of any age tend to be mere formulary productions in which nearly everything is determined by their writers' preoccupation with what the general public expected, or would resent, in writings of a certain kind. This historian must attempt to place himself in the points of view of his authors and try to understand their extraformal problems of this order, and their modes of solving these, in the light not necessarily of what contemporary playgoers and readers really were—which is always a somewhat vain inquiry—but of the images of them which his authors had formed and were guided by, insofar as these can be inferred from indications in their works, supplemented by such external evidence as is available. He will ask also, in the same connection, how far in the construction of particular works their writers appear to have deferred—often with formal or technical consequences one would not otherwise expect—to current critical prejudices or doctrines, and make an effort, when this is clearly the case, to locate the effects as exactly as possible in the constituent parts of the works. He will ask likewise what special traits of object, means, or manner in any work can be made fully intelligible only by a reconstruction of the particular occasion which inspired its writing: an excellent example of such inquiry is E. N. Hooker's study of Dryden's *Annus Mirabilis*.

He will consider, again—and for some works the question is of great importance—the relation to a poet's formal ends of the intrinsic or conventionalized character of the matter with which the author worked. The question includes but goes beyond the question of "sources" in the common philological sense. It arises whenever we know the "sources" of a work, literary and non-literary,

69

basic and incidental, and then ask what the consequences were, for the author's handling of the formal problems peculiar to the work, of his choice or invention of such and such a story or argument, such and such characters, such and such a mode of language or verse, such and such conventions of plot construction or representation, and so on. It seems clear, in general, that when an author has once committed himself to material decisions of this kind, even if they were determined originally by his conception of the desired form, he is thereafter limited, to a greater or lesser extent, in what he can do. The great difficulty is of course that any unqualified statements we may be tempted to make about the limitations inherent in this or that specific kind of matter are likely to be contradicted, sooner or later, by the achievement of some artist. Who would have thought in advance, for example, that Dostoevski could have made a great tragedy out of so inferior a plot formula, theoretically considered, as that of *The Brothers Karamazov?* A writer can say of two subjects that one seems to him more promising or interesting than the other, but that means merely that he happens to see more possibilities of doing something with it; and he is therefore an uncritical historian who ventures to argue from the fact that a work is, or appears to him to be, artistically unsuccessful to the conclusion that this was due to the author's choice of subject or his decision to write within the conventions of a certain verse form or literary genre. An extreme instance is J. M. Robertson's argument that Shakespeare was necessarily condemned to failure in his effort to achieve unity of character in *Hamlet* because of the intractable nature of the "plot" he took over from the old play; as if, in the first place, he did fail and as if, in the second place, the difficulties Robertson points out could not have been overcome, within a certain range of invention, even by a dramatist of much less genius!

The problem, nevertheless, is a real one and, to a historian who approaches it in a less a priori spirit, one susceptible, frequently, of illuminating solutions. It is obviously easier for writers to see artistic possibilities of a certain kind in certain subject matters at one moment in history rather than at another; for example, the difficulties involved in getting serious emotional effects out of materials once appropriated to comedy are certainly less arduous at present than they were at the beginning of the century. It is a great advantage to

70

an original artist also, as Eliot has remarked, if the "form" in which he proposes to write has already been extensively cultivated by his contemporaries and immediate predecessors, since in that case much of his work of material or technical invention has already been done. (It is of course true that some artists have thought this a disadvantage and that there is, besides, for any given art, a point beyond which the development of its conventions tends to yield diminishing returns, although we can perhaps never know beforehand when this point has been reached.)

The historian will not neglect such considerations in his attempts to reconstruct the circumstances in which particular works were composed, but he will also be able, occasionally at least, to show in more concrete ways how what writers did or failed to do was influenced by the matter they used. It is not hard, for instance, to trace the partial failure of Stevenson's *The Master of Ballantrae* (a failure which every one, including the author, has noted) to his inability to fuse together the two emotionally somewhat discrepant stories out of which its fable was built. And it requires no very sophisticated analysis, again, to see that, as between *Othello* and *Macbeth* and *Julius Caesar* and *Coriolanus,* the given plot materials of the earlier plays in each pair were such as lent themselves much more readily to the effect of tragic pity and fear which Shakespeare apparently desired to produce, in some degree, in all four plays—for example, they demanded much less in the way of choral and representational assistance for the sake of keeping the opinions and emotions of the audience in the right artistic line than did the given plot materials of the other two.

It is possible, finally, to say of any literary work that it would undoubtedly have been different from what it is had its author been in a different psychological state at the time of its inception and writing —had his mind been working more rapidly or sluggishly, had he been more absorbed in his task or more indifferent to it, more intent on doing something new or more content with repeating the kinds of things he had already done, or had luck been more with him or more against him in the moment when he conceived its design. The trouble is that, although such factors obviously help to determine the variations in artistic quality in successive works of the same kind by the same writer, there is little or nothing the historian can say about them over and above what is implied in his critical analyses of the works.

71

He can talk more easily, as many historians and biographers are fond of doing, about such accidents of production as where a certain work was composed or under what circumstances the idea for it occurred to the writer, and whether it was written rapidly or slowly, with much revision or little, without or with advice from wife, cook, publisher's reader, theater director, or friend, in longhand or on a typewriter, in sickness or in health, and so on. These things are undoubtedly also causes, and some of them have been made into recipes for literary success addressed to intending writers. The difficulty is to know how to deduce from such variables any of the literary effects exhibited by particular completed works and hence how to give them any other status in a literary history than that merely of interesting or trivial incidental facts. And although it seems that there ought to be a somewhat greater significance in the circumstance that some works (Pope's *Epistle to Dr. Arbuthnot* is an example) were put together finally out of fragments originally composed with quite different ends in view, it is usually impossible, here again, to find acceptable premises in terms of which the causal connections can be made.

Perhaps I have said enough, however, about the kinds of extra-poetic causes that may immediately affect, in ways more or less susceptible of historical investigation, the outcomes of particular acts of literary construction. Taken by themselves apart from the influence necessarily exerted by the intended form, they are obviously capable of explaining only the presence and material character of certain of the elements of subject matter and technique which an author has invented or borrowed in conceiving and writing a given work. They are essential to a full understanding of what was done, but such understanding is possible only when the historian concentrates in the first instance on the artistic causes of a work and then estimates in relation to these the other causes stemming either from the author's extraformal aims or from the conditions set for him by his conception of his audience of readers or critics, the occasion of his writing, the peculiar nature of his materials, and his personal situation at the time. The convergence of verifiable statements involving the interrelation of factors of all three types will bring us as close as we can get to the sufficient immediate causation of a literary work, and the same criterion of causal adequacy will guide the historian in his explanatory generalizations, at this level, concerning the various works of a given author, a given school, or a given period.

A similar relation holds—given the premises of the narrative history of forms—between this whole group of three proximate constructional causes and the more remote, preconstructional causes of literary events as holds between the artistic causes of a particular work and the other two immediate causes just discussed. Of preconstructional causes the least remote, it goes without saying, is the author himself; it is only as mediated through him that the general or collective causes of literary change can produce their effects in works, and it is only in him, as a continuing substrate of abilities, habits, memories, feelings, interests, and aims, that the immediate particular causes of these effects can operate. He is an individual man, and hence can never be sufficiently explained as a product of the society or culture in which he acts—except in that mode of history which substitutes relationships of participation for causes and effects. He is also, insofar as he interests the literary historian, a maker of works of art, and hence never, considered merely as a man, a sufficient cause—except again on some theory of organic participation—of the particular works he creates. These are distinct from him as he is distinct from his age or the literary and intellectual traditions to which he attaches himself: there is nothing in what we know, or can learn, about the life, personality, education, reading, moral convictions, or literary theories of Fielding, for example, by which we can make intelligible causally, without other principles, either the peculiar artistic synthesis achieved in *Tom Jones* or the formal differences between that novel and *Amelia*.

It is necessary to insist on this obvious point since its implications have seldom been acted on by historians even of the most literal kind. But having done this we may proceed to the converse, and not less obvious, truth, that the productive acts of any writer, however original and unpredictable in advance even by the writer himself, nevertheless presuppose as their necessary conditions characteristics of the man, as an individual molded by and molding the circumstances of his career, which the historian may investigate independently of his inquiries into the immediate causes of the writer's works. He may

73

uncover thus, depending upon the availability of documents, an indefinite number of biographical facts; his problem is to know which of these have causal relevance in the literary history he is constructing. It is clearly not the same problem for him as for the writer of a literary biography as such a work is usually conceived, nor can he solve it, in the manner of many literary historians in other modes, by falling back on the easy formula *sa vie et ses oeuvres*. He is writing a narrative history of forms designed to make intelligible the successive achievements of writers in relation to concurrent changes in formal ends and in the artistic devices and conventions of material used in actualizing them in works; and his principle of continuity is therefore something distinct from and over and above the particular careers of the authors whose individual accomplishments and whose functions as agents or signs of change he has to account for. Accordingly, his criteria for the selection and arrangement of biographical facts must be extrabiographical; that is to say, his guide in each instance must be his prior knowledge of what an author's achievements were in themselves, as concrete wholes distinguished by such and such material and technical accidents, and of what their relation was, as events productive of more or less extensive or significant innovations in form, matter, or technique, both to one another and to earlier and contemporary works by other authors in the same kinds. Knowing these things, he can then reason back from them to the biographical conditions and happenings which made them possible insofar as these can be connected by reasonable premises with particular characteristics of the writer's productions. In short, he will proceed from the works to the man, as what at this stage of his inquiry is less well known, and his method will consequently be the reverse of that favored by many modern biographical critics, who begin by conjecturing the nature of an author's private interests, moral problems, or childhood fixations, from his letters or other records, and then resolve his literary works, often on Freudian assumptions, into necessary consequences or signs of these.

The biographical causes thus arrived at will inevitably be multiple in kind, ranging from the author's native powers and temperament, through the diverse formative influences exerted upon him by the social, cultural, and religious circumstances of his family, by his youthful experiences, education, and reading, and by his methods of earning a living, to his development of personal convictions about morals, politics, or art, his decisions as between different literary kinds and traditions, his chance encounters with persons and books, and the effects on him of public events of one kind or another during the course of his career. From the point of view of the historian's problems these causes will fall into two classes: those which account for the likenesses between an author's works, however progressively different these may be, and the literary or ideological traditions in which he was working; and those which account for his divergences, in both kind and quality of achievement, from past or contemporary practice. The historian's method is such that it is much easier for him to do justice to causes of the first type than to those of the second, whether the effects to be explained are the writer's choices of forms or shifts from one form to another, his selection and elaboration of subjects, his uses of certain techniques rather than others, or his preferences in language and verse. In all these respects, if comparison is possible at all, it is simple enough to point out lines of filiation with earlier or contemporary literature and thought, some of which at least can be established as probable cases of direct borrowing, reminiscence, imitation, emulation, or influence, and, on the basis of an accumulation of such cases for the various works of an author, to generalize to his character as a representative figure in a movement or age.

It would be absurd to minimize the value for literary history of this kind of information, which the techniques of philological scholarship are peculiarly well fitted to uncover. But it would be equally absurd to suppose that it can give us, taken by itself, more than a part of the story—a very small part, indeed, for any writer of more than ordinary originality and power. Such a writer, as we have said, is by definition, and antecedently to the writing of any particular work, a man who cannot help altering more or less, at the same time that he assimilates, the ideas and materials of his age and the traditions of art he has elected to follow. The historian of forms, while not neglecting the question of sources, will thus seek to handle it in such a way as to make clear the extent to which a given writer is himself a cause as well as an effect of the influences playing upon him. He will observe, for example, that though Fielding's moral doctrine, as set forth explicitly in his essays and used in various ways in his novels, has an obvious affinity with the doctrines of numerous divines since the days of his favorite Barrow, it yet takes on a form of its own when viewed in the light not merely of its elements and catchwords but of the particular patterns of arguments which define it in Fielding's statements. The historian will be as much concerned with noting such transformations as with tracing the matters transformed to their origins in the writer's education, experience, or reading. He will attempt to exhibit the special features which differentiate a particular writer's response to a common influence from the responses of his contemporaries; he will emphasize the peculiar conjunctions of materials from heterogeneous sources which tend, even when the borrowings (as in Montaigne) are extensive, to set a writer of some originality of mind apart from others; above all, he will take pains to discriminate causally among instances of indebtedness or influence by showing how much, precisely, they explain in an author's works, that is, whether the debt to an earlier writer or tradition is for subject matter, or for suggestions in handling the medium, or for devices of technique, or for the structural formula of a plot or of certain incidents or characters, or for the idea, directly or indirectly imparted, of formal effects to be aimed at, or for some special combination of these possibilities. It is only when such distinctions have been made, for example, that we can say exactly what peculiar meaning "the manner of Cervantes" had for Fielding or what was characteristically Thomson's in his use of Newtonian ideas.

The ideal, in short, is to relate a writer's preconstructional assimilation of the various external influences that molded his habits of thought, feeling, and writing, or supplied him with particular materials and intentions, as closely as the data permit to the quality of inventiveness he displayed, successively in his different works, in solving the peculiar complexes of problems, never quite the same on any two occasions, which confronted him immediately in the composition of each. It is thus that the historian would proceed if his problem, for instance, was to make intelligible Pope's innovations in the couplet: having analyzed Pope's performance on the basis of an adequate literal prosody, he would attempt to interpret it in the light of converging inquiries into (1) the nature and extent of his adherence to and departures from previous practice, (2) his choices of earlier poems as models or as starting points for further developments, (3) his doctrines concerning versification as such independent of its uses, and the immediate and remote origins of these, (4) the nature of the problems of verse technique set for him generally by his decision to write didactic and satirical poems designed to affect a certain kind of audience by virtue both of their particular modes of argument and of the special qualities of moral character displayed by their speakers, and (5) the peculiar and differing poetic problems of this order presented by his successive poems.

Beyond such convergences of biographical and artistic causes it is perhaps impossible for the historian to go with any security in his attempts to explain the achievements of an author or his role in contributing to literary change. It is obvious that the writing of a notably original and powerful work or the discovery of a significantly new form presupposes genius as well as art and experience, but there is no way in which the historian can talk about a writer's genius apart from a critical analysis of his productions and it is seldom possible to reconstruct the process of invention by which a new form or technique was conceived. It is doubtless true that a writer who has something new to say will tend to seek a new form of expression, but this does not imply that another writer may not start with the intuition of a new form and then cast about for new matter to embody it in. There have been instances of both procedures, and the historian will not ordinarily be in a position to say, for a given instance, which was which. The extent, moreover, to which a writer departs from his predecessors or deviates from his own early manner will depend in large part on how impatient he is with doing merely what has already been done well or often—a spirit common to all artists, scientists, and scholars who, even if not geniuses, have succeeded in revealing fresh possibilities in their subjects. But here again there is nothing the historian can say that is not contained in his descriptions of the novel things achieved; the most he can do is to make clear whether the novelty was the result, in a given case, of a revolutionary rejection of the past or of a more or less thoroughgoing adaptation of traditional materials to new ends and uses. There will consequently always remain a margin of chance or mystery after the historian has done his best, and this will be true not only of the divergences of certain authors in the direction of greater artistic excellence or technical sophistication in a particular species of writing but of the lapses of others from the standards previously attained in works of writers well known to them or in earlier works of their own. The English tragic playwrights of the eighteenth century certainly included few men (if any) of notable dramatic talent, but this is scarcely a sufficient explanation of the fact that, although they knew Shakespeare well and wrote for audiences nourished on his tragedies, they yet neglected notoriously all the formal and technical lessons he might have taught them. And who will say that there is compelling necessity in any of the numerous attempts to account for the supposed artistic failure of *All's Well That Ends Well?*

4. The Same Subject Continued

The causal problems we have so far considered are relatively easy in comparison with those which arise when the historian of forms undertakes to make historically intelligible not merely the construction of individual works or the successive productive acts of individual writers but those larger changes in literary characteristics which manifest themselves in many works by many writers through a more or less extended period of time. Where is he to look for the causes of such great collective events as the rise and flourishing of Elizabethan drama, the development and decline of the "metaphysical" tradition in poetry, the general shift from mimetic to didactic, satirical, and occasional forms after the Restoration, the emergence of the novel of common life and then the Gothic romance in the eighteenth century, the Romantic movement, the new English and American poetry of the twentieth century? Or such less conspicuous yet in their way important things as the disappearance in the later seventeenth century of the older conventions of court poetry, or the increasing interest of dramatists at this time in serious plots turning on alternatives of choice for the hero or heroine neither of which could bring happiness, or the slowness of the early novelists to adapt to their uses the techniques of dialogue available to them in drama, or the greater success of eighteenth-century writers with comic than with serious forms, or the shift in didactic poetry, between the eighteenth and nineteenth centuries, from a primary concern with moral philosophy to a primary concern with philosophies of nature, or the modern taste, in serious fiction, for plots of disillusionment or frustration, with bewildered or fearful protagonists?

There are endless causal problems of these sorts, for many of which variant solutions have been suggested or insisted upon by historians of other schools: all of these the historian of forms will consider and some of them he will be able to use. Success in finding "explanations" for general literary developments or changes has been greater, of course, in proportion as historians have looked not for causes in the literal sense but for correspondences or correlations based upon analogies of characteristics—as, for instance, between difficult techniques of contemporary poetry and the methods of modern science or the disappearance of formerly common beliefs from modern life. The analytical commitments of the historian of forms prevent him, fortunately or unfortunately, from utilizing such easily manipulated explanatory devices. He can consider as causes of the highly particularized literary effects he is trying to make intelligible only those events or changes which he can connect with the literary effects by showing their direct or indirect operation, as humanly likely conditions or stimuli, on the intellectual, moral, and literary habits and aims and, through these, on the productive acts of the writers in questions; so that, for example, if the Industrial Revolution is proposed as a major cause of Romantic poetry, he will want to be shown in precisely what ways the language, rhythms, imagery, thought, character, situations, and effects of the great body of Romantic poems would necessarily or probably have been different had the Industrial Revolution not occurred. And he can discover causes in this sense, as we have frequently said before, only by reasoning back to them from the literary facts or changes which are to be explained; by looking, that is, for those antecedent things or conjunctions of things without which they could not in all likelihood have come about or come about thus and not otherwise, with this rapidity or to this extent, at this time, in this place.

The first prerequisite to any search for collective causes in the history of forms is therefore such an analysis of the literary ingredients of the development under consideration as was outlined in the second section of this essay. The historian, in other words, must be clear to begin with as to exactly what it is he is trying to explain: whether its full definition (as in the case of the major literary events mentioned above) entails more or less complex discriminations of formal ends, materials, and techniques and of the varied interrelationships of these in many works, or mainly distinctions appropriate to materials

79

or techniques; and whether the facts to be accounted for with respect to any or all of these variables are chiefly facts of persistence or chiefly facts of change, and, if the latter, whether the change was gradual or sudden, piecemeal or wholesale, a change of kind (as the emergence of a new poetic species) or only a change in quality or in extent of activity relative to a species or a number of species already in the tradition.

There is in the history of forms no other principle of relevance than this for the judgment of what causes, among those the historian may think of looking for, he ought to consider seriously and what he ought to reject. The judgment will ever be a delicate one, since the causal explanations offered by a history, whatever its subject matter, can never be framed in terms of general laws but must always remain hypotheses, chosen in preference to other possible hypotheses about why something happened, merely because of their arguably greater power of rendering the particulars in the history intelligible.

The best, therefore, that the historian of forms can do is to see to it that any general causal suppositions he may advance conform as closely as the data permit to the several criteria which the experience of historians and of practical men has indicated for inquiries of this kind.

The first of these is clearly sufficiency of explanation, and for the literary historian this implies two things: negatively, that he will proceed on the principle that wherever, as in any instance of collective change, multiple literary variables—formal, material, technical—are involved, the causes will likewise be multiple; and, positively, that in his interpretations he will seek to conjoin propositions about all the factors necessarily present in the kind of change he is dealing with. He will thus recognize that we understand any human event or development most fully when, given a sequence of happenings of a certain order, we know (a) the specific purposes which animated the agents and determined their problems, (b) their individual characters, backgrounds, habits, and ideas, and (c) the nature of the antecedent situation, as they saw it, out of which came the actions by which they altered it in such and such respects.

The second criterion is equally obvious: it is simply that the causes proposed must be appropriate to the effects they are intended to clarify, that is, they must possess the capacity, mediately or immediately, to bring about results of the particular kinds in question. We may suspect, thus, at least until some one shows the chain of intervening steps more convincingly than has been done, that the special constitution of the audiences in the private theaters of London *ca.* 1608 is an inappropriately assigned cause of the "romantic" tendencies displayed in the dramas written for these theaters by Shakespeare and Fletcher. The standard literary histories are full of causal conjectures concerning which the same doubts may be felt; the best remedy against them is a prior inquiry, such as the historian of forms will always undertake, into the immediate artistic causes of the works they are supposed to explain.

The final criterion is commensurateness: causes are incommensurate when they are either too particular or too general, in their nature and probable efficacy, relative to the extent or complexity of the phenomena they are used to account for. Of the first sort are the current clichés about the effect of the Royal Society on the general development of prose style after 1660, the influence of Hobbes's psychology of the imagination on the rise of Augustan poetry and taste, the contribution of Shaftesbury to the formation of "sentimentalism," and, more notoriously still, the tyranny of Rousseau over the European Romantic movement; it is perhaps not unfair to add that the sin of incommensurateness in this first sense has been cultivated with peculiar assiduity by the devotees of "comparative literature" in the usual narrow meaning of that term. Of incommensurateness in the second sense many illustrations will doubtless suggest themselves, such as a recent attempt to explain the contrast between Pope's "love of conciseness" and the preference of most nineteenth-century poets for a more distended manner of writing by positing as the main cause the greater leisure prevalent in the eighteenth century as compared with the later period; as if this same cause did not operate also on such contemporaries of Pope as Thomson and Young, who were far from loving, or at least manifesting, "conciseness."

These are general criteria, and their proper application to questions of causality in the history of forms requires that the historian keep in mind also a number of other distinctions. The facts to be explained at this stage of his inquiry, as we have said, are those presented by the spectacle of many writers of varied origins, characters, and outlooks exploiting, simultaneously or successively, a certain range of materials and techniques to the end of making literary works of certain more or less clearly differentiable kinds; and causal problems distinct from those involved in the analysis of individual works and authors necessarily arise for the historian whenever he is confronted by collective similarities and differences either in the literary species cultivated by his writers or in their choices of materials or in their preferences in techniques. The great temptation in such cases is to assume that since the facts are general—that is, statable in terms of generalizations from numerous particular acts—the causes must also be general, in the sense of involving collective stimuli operative on the writers as a group. The prevalence of this assumption accounts, at least in part, for the inclusion in most literary histories of descriptive chapters or sections on the "background" of the literature of a period or of one of its branches, setting forth much miscellaneous and not always strikingly relevant information concerning political habits and activities, social conditions, the state of education and learning, the tastes of the general public, the major movements of ideas, the development of science, the circumstances governing publication, and so on. This is much less misleading, however, than the equally common propensity of historians to suppose that the occurrence of a large and complex literary development, such as the revolution in English poetry after the middle of the seventeenth century, must remain a mystery unless some similarly large and complex development in another sphere of contemporary life, such as, in this case, "Rationalism" or "Materialism" or "the Newtonian world view," is asserted to be its essential cause.

The historian of forms will be skeptical of such hypotheses (if they are indeed hypotheses and not, as surely in many histories, *geistesgeschichtliche* analogies based on mythical constructions of the history of ideas) on the ground that they beg the question of causes by discouraging adequate inquiry into the more immediate factors, both formal and extraformal, which necessarily operate in literary production. He will ask—to go with the same illustration—whether a sufficient or nearly sufficient understanding of what happened in English poetry after 1650 may not be arrived at by a process of adding together the various proximate causes he has discovered, so that a telling of the detailed story of why poet after poet from before the Restoration into the eighteenth century chose the particular forms, materials, and techniques he did would by itself go far toward making the collective changes intelligible. However this may be, he will at least recognize the possibility, familiar to all who have studied in local detail the mechanism of general elections, that an outcome statable in common terms does not inevitably presuppose, as its decisive cause, common antecedents in the opinions, interests, and actions of individuals.

He will give due weight, therefore, to causes of this additive or coincidental type, but without minimizing the importance, where this can be established, of collective causes of various kinds. In dealing with these he will be careful to differentiate, in the first place, between causes in the positive sense of influences or stimuli tending in a certain direction and causes in the more negative sense of antecedent and environing conditions. The latter may be either literary or non-literary, and of these the first are ordinarily much the easier to handle. We can thus say that the popular English drama of the late sixteenth century would not have been what it was except for the peculiar character of the earlier dramatic developments, although the most complete analysis of these is not in itself sufficient to explain the forms the new drama took; or that the directions followed by English poetry after about 1914 would certainly have been different had it not been for the distinctive poetic tendencies of the Edwardians; and we can make many similar propositions connecting particular literary changes with the state of literature in general or of some species of literature or of some tradition of materials or techniques or of the language in general or the literary language or the language of poetry or the language of tragedy, at the time when the change began. It is of course indispensable to do this; the difficulty is to distinguish between what the antecedents were in themselves—that is, as analyzed objectively in their own terms—and what they appeared to be to the writers involved in the change, since it is obviously only in an account of the latter aspect that their causal relevance to what happened becomes clear.

The same principle holds for the treatment of non-literary conditions, although here it is much harder to trace the connections. We can assert as a general rule—or at least many historians have done so —that certain political, moral, economic, social, or intellectual circumstances are more stimulating or more discouraging to literary activity or to literary activity of a certain kind than others; with greater probability we can say the same thing about modes of literary patronage, situations in the theater or book trade, and changes in the composition and tastes of readers; but we know from our experience and observation that objective facts of this order are likely to be interpreted differently by different writers and consequently to be followed by actions often quite unpredictable in terms of the rules: the most ample provisions for encouraging learning do not always give us learned men, nor does the badness of an educational program mean that all the students who suffer under it will get a bad education. The point, of course, cannot be pushed too far: it is difficult, for instance, to conceive of a flourishing drama in a society which has banished the stage. The historian, however, is not apt to go astray in such cases; his besetting temptation is to find not too little but too much causal significance in the known antecedent or concomitant circumstances of literary change, and he can be easily deceived into oversimple explanations, especially of revolutionary or reformist movements in literature, by what the actors in such movements say about the immediate past and the obstacles it interposed between them and desirable new achievement.

A case in point is the new American literature of the 1920's as represented by such men as H. L. Mencken, Van Wyck Brooks, F. Scott Fitzgerald, Ernest Hemingway, Sinclair Lewis, and Ezra Pound. The movement is often treated, somewhat naively, as if it came about in spite of the restrictive moral and cultural conventions, the deadening standards of the colleges and magazines, the tyranny of the sanctified older reputations which, as its exponents insisted countless times, had thwarted originality in the United States since the Civil War. These men were certainly justified in attacking American culture as they saw it, and their revolt led to much excellent new writing. The historian, however, before making too much of their courage in breaking with the old bad traditions, will be inclined to ask whether this very badness was not actually, for them, rather a rich opportunity than an unfortunate impediment; for what, after all, would Mencken have been without his Bible Belt and his Van Dykes and Mabies, or Lewis without his Main Street, or Pound without the Y.M.C.A.?

The inquiry concerning conditions thus leads into the inquiry concerning causes in the stricter sense; and here again the historian will distinguish between relatively general and relatively particular causes and, among the latter, between those more and those less immediately determinative of the constructive choices of writers and hence of the formal differences of literary works. Out of the many particular causes of the first sort to which historians have rightly attached importance we can mention only a few. Any list would include, obviously, the kind of happenings which, when they take place on a large scale, we call renaissances: the gradual or sudden shifts of interest that bring back into prominence, as exemplars of form or technique or as sources of literary materials, works or writers of whole literatures of the past—the new studies of Virgil in the twelfth century, the successive waves of enthusiasm for Greek models from the fifteenth century to the nineteenth, the Celtic and Scandinavian revivals of the eighteenth century, or the "return to Donne" of our own day. There have been few literary historians of any school who have not attempted to do justice to such phenomena, although we could often wish for greater particularity in the analysis both of the peculiar values in the revived authors which different writers or generations selected for admiration and of the special artistic uses to which these were put in new works. Justice has also been done more or less adequately to a second type of cause which is in a way the counterpart of this: the power of successful new works or authors to inspire imitation, adaptation, or parody among contemporary writers at home and abroad—we need consider only how much has been written about the "schools" of such writers as Chaucer, Spenser, Donne, Jonson, Milton, Wordsworth, and Scott, or how freely contemporary Continental novelists have acknowledged the stimulus of Hemingway and Faulkner.

Somewhat less attention, perhaps, has been given to a third type of cause, closely related to this, which William Minto was tempted to erect into a kind of law: the peculiar power of attracting literary talent which seems to be inherent in new and developing "forms" in the generation after their discovery. "The stimulating novelty of the form," writes Minto, "must stand first in the list of 'causes' of the greatness of Elizabethan drama. The significance of this simple fact, as generally with obvious facts, has been overlooked by aetiological speculators." Both the Greek and the English drama, he notes, attained their height within a generation of their birth, and subsequent efforts to revive their magnificence have proved unsuccessful. "To put it somewhat mathematically, in the first generation of their existence they drew towards them irresistibly a larger proportion of free intellect than they were ever able to attract in subsequent generations. This is the law of all subjects of disinterested intellectual effort, whether artistic or scientific. The most ambitious intellects rush after the newest subjects with which they have affinity: if the subjects are great, and succeed in fascinating congenial minds, then the results are great." Properly qualified, as Minto qualifies it in his final sentence, this is clearly a valuable insight, verifiable in the experience of most of us; it has the advantage, furthermore, of suggesting a realistic causal hypothesis for the interpretation of large collective facts which have often been treated, somewhat mystically, as instances of the imagination or sensibility of an age finding its most effective and characteristic expression.

The converse of this species of cause has been much more frequently invoked, though usually without sufficient attention to its positive implications: the strong urge to change which is normally felt by ambitious or original minds when they become convinced, for good or bad reasons, that the possibilities of a particular form, technique, or body of materials have become exhausted as a result of either much or outstandingly successful cultivation; as when Dryden remarked of the Elizabethan dramatists that there is "scarce an Humour, a Character, or any kind of Plot, which they have not us'd" and added that this is "a good Argument to us either not to write at all, or to attempt some other way." It is not hard for the historian to discover evidence in nearly every literary generation of the existence of such feelings; the difficult thing is to find sufficient reasons for the particular choices of "some other way" which the writers made.

There are at least three directions in which the historian may look. He may ask whether the suggestion might not have come from abroad, as in Eliot's attempt to renew English poetry by borrowing technical devices already developed to a high degree of sophistication in the French Symbolist tradition. Or he may inquire whether the renewal—of poetry, for instance—might not have been effected by importing subjects, techniques, or forms from another literary species, such as the essay or the novel; it is thus that Minto accounts for much that was new and apparently revolutionary in the poetry of Cowper,

Wordsworth, Scott, and Byron; and in a similar way, perhaps the historian can find a partial explanation of the directions taken by the so-called "lyric revival" after 1740 by examining how far the characters, situations, thoughts, and emotions of the many short lyrics of this period exploited materials previously worked up in the episodes of large-scale didactic poems like Thomson's *Seasons*. Or he may consider, finally, in the manner suggested in the second section of this essay what were the theoretical possibilities of further innovation in a particular literary species at a particular time, given the stage of development which it had then reached, so that, for example, the various lines of specialization followed by writers of serious drama after Shakespeare or the so-called "breakup" of the novel in the generation after Richardson and Fielding become at least partly intelligible as natural, though not inevitable, next steps beyond what those masters had done.

All these are "literary" causes in the sense that they all involve factors the origin and efficacy of which lie within the relatively closed world of men specializing, as writers of poems, plays, novels, essays, and the like, in the production of literary works. The influence of literary criticism on literary practice clearly falls in the same class, especially in those periods when the doctrine and judgments of critics have had only a remote or indirect relation to the development of philosophy; the great exceptions have been the dialectical and "scientific" criticism, respectively, of Plato and Aristotle, the "philosophical" criticism of Hume, Burke, Kames, Dugald Stewart, and many others in the eighteenth century, the "transcendental" systems of Coleridge and the Germans, and the more recent efforts in speculative criticism of Croce and Dewey.

That the practice of writers in the different literary arts tends to be affected, more or less decisively, by contemporary or earlier formulations of the ends and appropriate devices and materials of these arts or of the principles of art in general and by the pronouncements of critics on the merits and faults of particular works is one of those general probabilities which no one ever thinks of denying but which few have been able to use convincingly in the causal interpretation of literary events. It has been a commonplace at least since David Hume that humanistic and social studies differ radically from the natural sciences in that their data are never immune from the formative or distorting influence of the theories set up to explain them. It is a much older commonplace that the forms of all the arts must first exist in the minds of artists before they can be embodied in works and hence must inevitably be subject to the pressure of whatever historically determined opinions the artists may hold as to how works of such and such kinds ought to be made. And anyone who has ever tried to write anything for publication knows how hard it is for an author, no matter how independent in spirit, to avoid altogether considering what critics and reviewers are likely to say of his performance. It seems to follow, therefore, that the relations between changes in literary production in any age and changes in critical theory and taste constitute one of the more pressing topics of causal inquiry for the literary historian.

And so indeed it must; the only trouble is the extraordinary difficulty which the problem presents, except now and then in the case of an individual work or writer, to the historian who wants to talk literally about causes and effects rather than analogically about correspondences and equations. For the peculiarity of the relationship between criticism and production is that the causes never run entirely in one direction. When a historian has discovered clear affinities between a particular body of literary works and the particular critical rules and criteria generally favored in the same age, he cannot always be certain how far the works are what they are because of the criticism and how far the criticism is what it is because of the works. Surely to some extent at least the writing of poetry in Britain and America since the 1920's has been directed as well as encouraged by the "new criticism" which emerged during the same period—there is probably more than malicious gossip, for instance, in the charge that a certain young poet has set himself deliberately to achieve Empsonian "ambiguity" in his verse. But it is hardly less certain that the "new criticism" itself, much of which has been written with the "new poetry" in view and with the promotion of a taste for such poetry as one of its objects, would not be exactly what it is had not the pioneers of the poetic renascence written as they did. This is one great difficulty. Another, scarcely less important, arises from the complementary fact that, although criticism may affect production and production criticism, the two activities remain distinct (even when the artists are also critics) by virtue of the operation in each of special causes or reasons foreign to the other. The critic, thus, may attempt to set forth principles for tragedy or the novel, and in doing so he will naturally be influenced by the tragedies or novels he has read or perhaps written, but he will also be influenced by the traditions of critical discussion itself and by the general premises of critical argument he has happened to choose. The artist, similarly, although his tragedies or novels may be affected by the criticism he has read or perhaps written, will tend to do as an artist, insofar as he is a good one, what his peculiar task and the traditions of his art indicate that he should do. There can be no easy or simple inferences, therefore, from the one field to the other, and the historian must always reckon with the possibility that in any period or in any writer, for this or another reason, the development of doctrine and the development of practice may follow quite divergent roads. The relations between the tragedies written in the eighteenth century, for example (some of them by men with considerable critical learning), and the statements of contemporary critics and theorists on what tragedy ought to be are by no means conspicuously close except on a few points; and anyone who argues from E. M. Forster's *Aspects of the Novel* to the principles of form which guided him in the composition of his own novels will have his eyes closed to a good part of the truth.

The historian of forms will show his awareness of these complexities in whatever he may say about the influence of critical ideas on the course of literary production. He will approach any possible influence of this kind from the point of view not of what he knows concerning the history of doctrines but of his prior analyses of the artistic problems which his writers faced because of their choices of formal ends. He will then ask how far such ends had been envisaged by critics or by the writers themselves as critics or makers of programs before they were embodied in works; as was the case, for example, with the "sublime ode," the pathetic novel of common life, and the tale of terror in the eighteenth century. He will raise similar questions, also, about changes in technique and conventions of material. How much critical discussion of French Symbolist devices, for instance, had taken place in England prior to the use of these or analogous techniques in English poems? Or what is the chronological relation of the turning away by poets of the eighteenth century from the standardized genres or of the "naturalistic" expansion of subject matter in the late

89

nineteenth-century novel or of the later concentration of novelists on "proletarian" or psychoanalytical themes to the development of theoretical sanctions for these departures? He will distinguish between those cases for which clear connections of cause and effect can be shown and those for which the telling of the prior critical story merely adds in a general way to the intelligibility of what the creative writers did. He will attempt likewise to distinguish, although this may not always be possible, among cases in which (a) the choice of a certain kind of "subject" was dictated by a desire to translate precepts of technique into practice, (b) cases in which, the "subject" having been chosen for reasons quite independent of doctrine, the character of its handling was affected, contrary to the peculiar needs of the form, by current critical teaching, and (c) cases in which, again given the "subject," the harmony of formal requirement and critical prescription was complete, so that the same thing would probably have been done even if no critic had written. The history of the unities of time and place in drama from the sixteenth century to the present day will supply illustrations of all three of these possibilities. He will also consider, in tracing the influence of a particular writer or work on subsequent production, the extent to which this influence was encouraged, impeded, or directed to certain aspects of the achievement rather than to others by the mediating effects of the critical discussions which the work or writer inspired; it should be possible to explain in these terms, at least partly, such things as the nature and course of Henry James's impact on later fiction or the differences between the eighteenth- and early nineteenth-century uses of Spenser. And there are, lastly, the interesting negative cases in which the development of literary production during a certain period has gone beyond or counter to or at any rate has proceeded more or less independently of the development of theory: such was the coincidence in the Renaissance of a rich imaginative literature dominated by imitative ends with critical schools which, however they differed in other traits, agreed in making the controlling purpose of poetry didactic.

The historian of forms will construct his narrative in such a way as to give due prominence to these situations along with the various more positive situations distinguished above; and since the causes of such varying relationships between criticism and practice are likely to be found, as I have said, quite as much in the evolution of criticism as in that of production, he will be led to a somewhat different treatment of the history of criticism from that ordinarily given in literary histories of the traditional types. It will be a treatment which, while making clear the material content of the doctrines and judgments set forth in critical writings and their relation to past or contemporary literary works, will take into account also the distinctive problems the critics were trying to solve and the peculiar assumptions and methods which conditioned the formulation and solution of these. The critical treatises and essays, in short, will be analyzed formally in their own terms no less than the poems and dramas they may have influenced, and their doctrines interpreted in the light of the specific and often widely variant ends and dialectical requirements so revealed. Only after this has been done can the historian feel safe in attributing any particular common positions to the critics of a given period (no matter how similar verbally their statements may be) or say with precision what significance for literary production is to be attached to any of the large critical "movements" (such as neoclassicism) which historians have loved to create.

We come finally to those causal factors the importance of which for the historian arises from the fact that the world of literary creation is after all only relatively a closed one: the audiences writers seek to interest usually lie altogether or in great part outside its bounds, and the writers themselves participate in varying ways and degrees in the esthetic, intellectual, and practical activities of their society and age, not necessarily as artists but as men.

There is less need to dwell on these factors than on some others. They have constituted, as we have tried to indicate, the special province of those literary historians who have sought to integrate literature dialectically with other things and for whom the most revealing explanations of what writers did lie not in their immediate activities and tasks as artists but in the "underlying" or "ultimate" causes of their behavior as men. The result has been to import into literary history a vast amount of discussion of the relations between literature and the other fine arts, literature and the evolution of ideas, and literature and society. The discussion has not always—has seldom indeed—been strikingly competent when judged by the best standards of the various specialized disciplines which have been drawn upon for materials, and the conceptions of extra-literary history thus disseminated have been typically doctrinaire and oversimple.

The problem, however, has been clearly posed, and we may therefore confine ourselves to noting a few of the respects in which the treatment of causes of this kind by the narrative historian of forms will differ from their treatment by historians of other schools. The historian of forms, of course, is concerned primarily with literal distinctions among works and the causes of these in terms of the character of the works as artistic syntheses. The consequences of this difference in approach can be seen most easily perhaps in his handling of the connections between literature and the other arts.

It has become a widespread fashion to talk about literary works by means of technical concepts borrowed from music, painting, architecture, and gardening, with the result that many poems and novels have been said to have a "symphonic structure" or to contain instances of "spatial form." It has been remarked, for example, that a poem of Pope, with "its collocation of a certain number of balanced or contrasted units . . . resembles architecture—houses built by Kent or palaces built by Wren"; and another scholar has undertaken to show the remarkable correspondences between the verse movement of Augustan poetry and the symmetries of the contemporary formal garden and then the equally remarkable similarity of the blank verse of Thomson and others to the more sinuous lines of the later English garden, the "antagonism" of the two styles signifying, naturally, a deep transformation in the spirit of the age. For the historian of forms such analogies can be starting points only; insofar as they are not merely lazy substitutes for a poetic analysis of the devices in question, they may suggest problems to him which he might not otherwise have seen; in dealing with these, however, he will proceed on the assumption that the causes of any apparently similar effects in two arts which differ radically in their media and their principles of construction must necessarily be distinct, and he will not be content until he has traced these in terms appropriate literally to each of the arts. The result may very well be, as in most or all of the examples just given, the simple conclusion that the analogy tells us more about the critic's or historian's method than

92

it does about any actual connections of cause and effect between the two arts. This will, of course, not always be true. Apart from the many ways in which writers have exploited their knowledge of the other arts in inventing subjects, descriptions, metaphors, and the like, and apart from the frequent close relations between poets, and musicians and between dramatists and designers of scenes, we know that the theories of literature prevalent in certain periods have tended to assimilate it more or less closely, in its general ends, to other arts. Sometimes, as in the eighteenth century, this has been to the plastic arts, sometimes, as in the nineteenth century, to music; the consequences can occasionally be seen in the preferences of writers for certain genres or in their attempts to devise new techniques. We know also that some writers, especially in modern times, have deliberately tried to get effects of arrangement in individual works which they hoped would remind readers pleasurably of musical forms; and we know what uses have been made by certain contemporary novelists and playwrights of technical expedients borrowed from the cinema. All these relations are susceptible, the data permitting, of literal causal treatment; they will never, perhaps, explain very much in the history of literary forms, but they will at least make the historian's narrative somewhat more intelligible here and there than it would have been had he neglected to take them into account. And there may be some advantage, in histories embracing the whole range of literary activity during a given period, in the kind of subsidiary reference to the state of the other arts— without either systematic analogizing or strict causal commitment —which George Sherburn, for instance, has employed in his account of the Restoration and eighteenth century; the illumination of the literary facts is indirect but surely not for that reason to be contemned.

The special uses which the historian of forms will make of what it is customary nowadays, thanks very largely to the influence of A. O. Lovejoy, to call the history of ideas cannot be so easily defined. The difficulties are due, in the first place, partly to the great variety of things covered by that term. The history of ideas has been made to include the formal treatment of principles and doctrines in the systems of philosophers and scientists; the independent development, in application to problems in many fields, of concepts or analytical

93

devices which, having been used in the construction of systems, have then passed into general currency as commonplaces of argument (for example, Plato's list of virtues, Aristotle's four causes, Newton's "universal attraction," Freud's libido); the shifting history of crucial or influential philosophic terms ("Nature," for instance); the persistent disputes over the relative importance of the different sciences and of their systematic relations to one another (as the numerous quarrels over the comparative values of natural and moral philosophy and the current attempts of Weizsäcker and others to rebuild physics on a historical model); the complex evolution, individually and in interrelation, of the arts of stating or arguing intellectual positions or persuading readers of their truth (for example, the Ramean "reform" of logic in the sixteenth century and the architectonic status given to rhetoric in the eighteenth); and, finally, the various institutions and other mechanisms by which ideas have been disseminated or transmitted from one culture or one generation to another.

The history of ideas, being itself a philosophic discipline, has naturally been affected by these many sources of variation in its subject matter, and the task of the literary historian who wishes to utilize its contributions is therefore complicated, in the second place, by the necessity of interpreting these in the light of the philosophic principles which have determined their formulation in the history. For the attribution of ideas to philosophers and others by the historian of ideas is never a simple matter of first discovering and then stating "facts" (as many of the literary historians who have drawn their notions of Elizabethan cosmology from Lovejoy or of eighteenth-century deism from Leslie Stephen have naively supposed). The character and significance of a given philosophic system or doctrine or of the ideological currents of a given age as represented in a history is inevitably conditioned quite as much by the historian's peculiar philosophic and methodological assumptions as by what is said in his texts. The predicament of the historian of ideas is indeed closely parallel to that of the historian of imaginative literature, so that it is possible to distinguish in the history of ideas three fundamental ways of approaching problems which correspond broadly to the three modes of literary history defined above: first, a grammatical way, characterized by the use of philological devices of exegesis and comparison for the sake of restating the explicit content of doctrines, grouping them chronologically and with respect to their topical bases, and explaining on historical grounds their dissemination and influence (for example, Thomas Stanley's *History of Philosophy* and F. T. H. Fletcher's *Montesquieu and English Politics*); second, a dialectical way, characterized by the use of general philosophic concepts and distinctions, not necessarily those of the historical texts, for the sake of ordering a sequence of doctrines or of exhibiting the basic affinities and oppositions in the ideas of an age (for example, in their very different fashions, Stephen's *English Thought in the Eighteenth Century*, Irving Babbitt's *Rousseau and Romanticism*, and Lovejoy's *The Great Chain of Being*); and third, a way, lacking as yet any very good name, the essence of which is a consideration of philosophic or scientific writings, separately and in sequence, in terms of their distinctive assumptions, problems, and ends and of the specifically different modes of argument by which their conclusions were reached and ordered (for example, the historical essays of Richard McKeon). Of these three modes of constituting the history of ideas, only the first and—increasingly in recent years—the second have had an appreciable influence on the treatment of ideas by literary historians. The historian of forms, however, will profit most from the methods appropriate to the third approach, since these alone are capable of giving him a view of intellectual history which neither obscures the literal meanings of doctrines nor separates these from their limiting and differentiating contexts of problems and ends; a view, moreover, which preserves the broad traditions of human thought and the historical interrelations of its divers fields without imposing a unity on any of its chronological phases such as we know from experience with contemporary ideas could never, in a literal sense, have existed.

The problem is further complicated, no matter how the content or method of the history of ideas is understood, by the fact that the relations between it and the history of imaginative literature may be investigated in two clearly distinct ways. The historian may start from an idea or a complex of ideas as better known and argue to the character and extent of the influence these had on literary works, or he may start from the literary works considered in their concrete wholeness and argue to the intellectual events or changes which influenced their forms and upon which at the same time they imposed new forms. The first mode of procedure has been the commoner by far. It is the dominant method—to give only a few random examples representing a variety of approaches to the analysis of ideas—of such recent studies as Marjorie Nicolson's *Newton Demands the Muse: Newton's "Opticks" and the Eighteenth Century Poets;* Theodore Spencer's *Shakespeare and the Nature of Man* and the related works of Hardin Craig and E. M. W. Tillyard; J. W. Beach's *The Concept of Nature in Nineteenth Century Poetry;* McKeon's essay on poetry, philosophy, and rhetoric in the twelfth century in *Critics and Criticism;* to say nothing of numerous incidental passages in larger histories dealing with the reactions of poets, novelists, and dramatists to the "thought" of their time. It is, indeed, a natural method for the intellectual historian whose subject matter embraces poetic as well as theoretical works, even though he may not subscribe to Lovejoy's contention that "the interest of the history of literature is largely as a record of the movement of ideas." For the literary historian, however, who is certainly not likely to agree with this thesis, its use as a basic method of interpreting artistic writings is subject to two serious limitations, one on the side of the inquiry into causes, the other on the side of the inquiry into effects. The latter is obvious enough: it is the danger that, since the continuum of his story is an intellectual rather than an artistic development, he will tend systematically to emphasize only those aspects of the "poetic" writings which can be seen as effects of the assumed cause, thus blurring or destroying altogether differences of artistic kind and hence of the internal causes affecting the poet's use of ideas, and reducing works of all species, even works of great poetic complexity, to a common denominator of simple dialectic or expression of belief, seldom much above the level of an essay by Seneca or Addison; the reader will think at once of many recent efforts to trace intellectual themes in Shakespeare. The other danger is slightly more subtle; it is the risk, which becomes especially great when the dialectical method is employed to constitute a "world view" for a period or to define a "tradition" of ideas, that the historian will attend to only those ideas in his literary texts and hence to only those intellectual causes among their antecedents which he can assimilate to his chosen subject. The reader will recall how many fresh things were seen in both James Thomson's poetry and his background once the influence of Newton was joined to that of Shaftesbury as a topic of investigation; and we may add that surprises still await the student of eighteenth-century literature who will take as his clue the easily demonstrated fact that the philosophical writings of Cicero were more intimately familiar to educated men in that age than most of the later writings which have commonly been treated as the foundation works of the Enlightenment.

The moral for the historian of forms is clear. He will continue to employ the approach through selected causes as a method of investigation, although he will define these literally rather than dialectically; and the retrospective causal sections of his narrative will often be strung on threads derived from the history of ideas, with literary works treated partially, as signs or evidence of intellectual change. These will be subordinate devices, however; the major continuum of his narrative will be literary rather than ideological, and his characteristic starting point in the causal consideration of ideas will accordingly be poems, novels, essays, and plays and the problems involved in the assumption or use by their writers of the same or different ideas for different or the same artistic ends. He must clearly be able to recognize and compare ideas, whether explicit or merely presupposed, when he comes upon them in works of these kinds, and this necessitates some competence in the techniques of intellectual as well as poetic analysis; but once the facts thus obtainable are clear for a given work, writer, or sequence of writings, the task of discovering and stating their causes will entail an inquiry in two stages, the first concerned with origins, the second with uses. The former will carry him back from literature to the history of ideas, only now with highly particularized questions in view which can never be satisfactorily answered in terms of clichés like "the Christian-humanist tradition," "the scientific spirit," "materialism," "rationalism," "antirationalism," "empiricism," "sentimentalism," and so on, and with an open mind as to where he may find the effective intellectual antecedents, if such there were, of the literary traits and changes he is concerned to explain. There are excellent models for researches of this type in some of the essays of Lovejoy and Etienne Gilson and in critical editions of texts such as F. B. Kaye's *Fable of the Bees*, P.-M. Masson's *Profession de foi du Vicaire Savoyard*, and André Morize's *Candide*. For the arguments and attitudes to which writers have given explicit statement in literary works the difficulties of the inquiry are no greater, and no less, than in any investigation of sources and traditions.

The really troublesome problems are those presented by the usually unexpressed assumptions about the beliefs and moral sentiments of the audience which underlie such things as an author's choice and development of a certain plot form or his supposition that certain acts or traits of character or modes of thinking will arouse sympathetic (or antipathetic) reactions. What conceptions of human nature, for example, were implied in the growing preference of eighteenth-century dramatists and novelists for plots, involving ordinary people, the peculiar pleasure of which was determined by the unexpected emergence, in the dénouement, of humane and generous feelings? It has usually been taken for granted that the appeal of such stories must depend on the prevalence of doctrines that insist optimistically on the essential "goodness" of average human nature, and various scholars, by a process of exegesis which has led to much distortion of the ideas of Shaftesbury, Steele, Rousseau, and others, have developed a causal interpretation of "sentimental" drama and fiction in these terms. But what if we argue, on the other hand—as can be done, I think, with much psychological plausibility—that our delight in manifestations of the social virtues, in literature or in life, is in direct proportion to our belief that such occurrences are rare? In that case, obviously, we should look for our causes not in the supposed moral "optimism" of the eighteenth century but in the somewhat more easily demonstrable pessimism of that period, or rather in its characteristic combination of pessimism about the motives from which men generally act with an ethical ideal that identified virtue more or less completely with "good-nature" and "tender generous feeling."

The second stage of the inquiry is the necessary complement of this, although I can think of only a few writings by literary historians in which its distinctive problems have been faced. These problems are set by the evident fact that ideas in literary works are what they are not only because of the circumstances, more or less external to literature, which have brought certain basic views about God, the universe, man, and philosophy, or certain special distinctions, doctrines, terms, methods, or modes of philosophic speech into prominence during a given time, but also, and no less decisively, because of the particular and highly differentiated functions which such materials may be made to serve in various kinds of works and in the various "parts" of any kind.

It seems simple enough, at first sight, to account for the ideas explicitly argued in a given philosophical poem or moral epistle by pointing to the author's adherence to such and such a school or tradition of thought; and this is about all that most literary historians have attempted in discussing works like the *De rerum natura,* the *Essay on Man,* or Thomson's *Seasons.* That the traditional ideas as stated in these works are never quite the same in interrelation, emphasis, and ordering as in the earlier works from which they were drawn is of course notorious. Apart from this, however, it makes a great difference, with respect to the status and causation of ideas in didactic writings of this sort, what the particular end of the poem is. It makes a difference whether the end is the setting forth of an argument as a statement of truth or whether the argument (as in Pope's poem) is a rhetorical means to the inculcation of an attitude toward the things in life to which the poem refers. We judge the value of the ideas by different standards in the two cases and hence we must judge differently concerning the reasons for their use— giving more weight in the first to the convictions of the author and more in the second to his notions of what readers were likely to believe.

So too with the various modes of allegory; although they all have a basis in doctrine, the causal relations between the doctrine and the poem are clearly not the same in the traditional allegories, like *Pilgrim's Progress,* which take for granted that the doctrine is known and generally accepted and in those more characteristically modern allegories, like some of Kafka's mythographic fables, in which a new and presumably difficult doctrine is being adumbrated through the symbolic devices of the work.

And there is a wide difference, which has seldom been sufficiently considered by historians, between the uses of intellectual materials in didactic writings of whatever kind and their uses in the construction of imitative dramas, narratives, and lyrics. Here the historian's problems fall into two groups: those involved in tracing the possible influence of earlier or contemporary ideological discussions, by the writers themselves as well as by others, on the invention of plot forms, episodes, characters, or character relationships (which is clearly not the same thing as inventing any of these for the sake of promoting the discussion); and those involved in accounting for what happened to the historically conditioned ideas when they entered into the "thought" of imitative works either as grounds of deliberation and reflection by the characters or as topics of choral or narrative commentary designed to enhance the effectiveness of the form vis-à-vis the audience. It is hard to see how there can be an adequate historical treatment of the effect of intellectual movements upon literature that does not recognize such differences as these and that does not attempt, in any clear case of influence, to assess the relative importance in the final result of the causes deriving at various removes from the history of ideas and causes deriving more immediately from the special natures of the artistic tasks which the writers faced in constructing their works.

Difficult as these problems are, they are yet relatively easy when compared with the problems facing the literary historian in his attempts to deal in a literal causal fashion with that vast congeries of possible causes of literary effects which is usually labeled, vaguely enough, "society." His common sense must tell him that the question is an important one—else how explain the prestige it has attained, in the minds of historians of all schools, since the eighteenth century? Common sense also tells him that if he is to investigate it with any intelligence or accuracy he must be trained not only in poetic, rhetorical, and intellectual analysis but in the various special disciplines which make up the "social sciences": he cannot get very far if he remains merely an amateur economist, an amateur sociologist, or an amateur political historian. Not many of the literary students who have had most to say about the relations of literature and society have been masters in any of these fields; what has kept the fact from becoming too glaringly apparent has been their reliance on a method of interpretation which makes analytical expertness in the non-literary subject matters they have annexed less essential than an ability to see and develop analogies from hints easily available to them in the writings of specialists. They have been encouraged in their efforts, moreover, by the apparently self-evident truth of the dogma that "literature is an expression of society." This dogma, as understood by most of its adherents, serves to guarantee the relevance of any collective circumstances in the background of literary production presenting correspondences with the works of the writers concerned. It is even better perhaps, as permitting greater dialectical neatness in the historian's exposition, if the background circumstances come to him already worked up speculatively into some species of myth (as in the works of Max Weber and R. H. Tawney on the relations between capitalism and the Protestant spirit or in the writings about the frontier in America by some of the disciples of Frederick Turner).

For reasons which I have often stated, the historian of forms is prevented, by the principles of his method, from falling back on these alluring expedients. He can have no wish to treat literature in abstraction from "life"; he can even conceive of it "as a part of the process of life itself," although he will not suppose that a poet or novelist ceases to "live" when he turns his mind away from politics or economics to concentrate on the problems of his art, or that to set literary works "firmly in a social context" means discussing them only or primarily in "social" terms. He will accordingly look for social causes, but he will know that a properly realistic (rather than metaphorical) comparison of literary with social phenomena requires that he have an independent knowledge of both and therefore a preliminary training which will at least qualify him to criticize on relevant scholarly grounds the conclusions and hypotheses of the experts in political and social history whom he consults. Moreover, his procedure being essentially an analytical one, he will be concerned only with those conditions or changes in the practical affairs of a society to which he is led by the necessity of accounting for traits in literary works and in the habits and ideas of writers which appear not to be adequately explicable in the light of more immediate causes. He will not assume that everything in literature—perhaps not even any of the more important things from his point of view—must have a "social" explanation if only he can find it, or that such an explanation, when found, can ever account fully for the particular effects that interest him. He will treat social causes, like all others, differentially, recognizing that whatever causes of this type he is able to establish will differ widely in significance, at different times or in different places, relative to other causes and to the aspects of literary works they help him to explain. He will keep in mind, above all, the peculiar difficulties that attend reasoning from cause to effect in this field. He will know, concerning any young writer at the outset of his career, how nearly impossible it is to infer correctly, from even the completest information about his political sympathies and his social and economic background, what the character and direction of his output will be as defined by any of the literary variables which are important for the historian of forms. So the best he can do, having examined the completed output in these terms, is to look to the writer's social background for any obvious sources of materials or stimuli in the light of which his works, in any of their aspects, can retrospectively be made more intelligible as events. And this process repeated for many writers will bring him as close as he can come, given the complexity of the subject and the futility of trying to explain particular happenings in terms of general statistical probabilities (such as the conclusions of sociologists respecting the behavior patterns of classes and other large groupings of men), to being able to set the collective facts of literature "firmly in a social context."

The relevance of such findings to his distinctive concerns as a historian of forms will vary greatly in degree of remoteness. In many cases the political or social events he is led back to will turn out to be only conditions sine qua non of literary change, important for the opportunities they opened up or closed off but for nothing much more positive than that. Such, for example, were the Norman Conquest, the Revolution of 1688, the achievement of freedom of the press, the spread of popular education in the nineteenth century, the emancipation of women, and the decline and fall, since 1900, of the older quarterly reviews. I have probably already said enough about how "causes" of this sort must be handled.

A second large class of events consists of those which can be shown to have had somewhat more positive but still very general effects on the state of mind both of writers and of broad sections of the public, so that new hopes or enthusiasms were generated or old illusions dispelled. Such, for example, were the religious struggles and changes of the sixteenth century, the French Revolution, World War I, and the rise of Soviet Russia. No one can doubt that events like

102

these have had an influence upon the spirit of literature at the times of their occurrence or at least upon the comparative fortunes of different writers with contemporary readers; the difficulty comes when the historian tries to discuss the influence in particular detail. As Minto shrewdly remarks of the supposed effects upon the rise of Elizabethan drama of the feelings generated by the triumph of Protestantism and the defeat of Spain, "one must have no small confidence in the power of general conditions over specific effects who would venture to say that our dramatists would never have come into existence, or would have sought some other line of activity, had Mary remained upon the throne instead of Elizabeth, and had England continued at peace with Spain"; it is hard to see "what the stir of the Reformation had to do with the dramatic tendencies of Marlowe, or how the defeat of the Armada was concerned in the migration of Shakespeare from Stratford to the London stage." The connection seems to be much clearer, at least on a superficial view, between the writings of the so-called "lost generation" of the 1920's and the moral impact of World War I; but leaving aside the fact that these writings were highly diversified in form, technique, and matter, can we be sure that they were not themselves as much a cause as an effect of the disillusionment commonly attributed to the war, or that *The Waste Land,* for instance, would not have been pretty much what it is had the war never occurred?

With a third type of events the historian is on safer ground; these are the happenings or changes to which it is possible to trace significant increments in the subject matter of literature or important shifts in the perspective from which old materials are viewed. Such, for example, in addition to some of the events already mentioned, were the geographical discoveries at the end of the Middle Ages, the opening up of America, the beginnings of intercourse with China, the conquest of India, the Industrial Revolution and its consequences, and, in this country, the Civil War, the Westward Movement, and the Great Depression. The literary effects of happenings of this kind, in bringing into prominence new stories, new scenes, new motives, new types of character, new objects of emotion, new words, are relatively easy to investigate, and they have not been neglected by scholars. Nevertheless, only a few of these (among them notably Gilbert Chinard in his three books on the myth of

America in French literature) have made a point of going beyond descriptions of the facts to the discussion in literary terms of the uses to which the fresh materials were put.

With a fourth class of events the difficulties for the historian of forms are much greater, but so also are the rewards. These events are the usually slow and gradual changes in social relationships and attitudes the effects of which can be discerned by comparing successive writers with respect to the propositions about such things which they appear to take for granted or think it necessary to insist upon. These include the social types or actions they choose for sympathetic or unsympathetic, serious or non-serious treatment and in general those traits of subject matter or emphasis which we would expect to be radically different in the works of authors living in and writing for (say) the semifeudal court society of the fourteenth century on the one hand and the largely democratic and semi-collectivist present-day world of the Labour Party and the New Deal on the other. The study of such characteristics is rewarding because it brings the historian fairly close to his writers' materials not in their raw state but as already partly formed for literary treatment. The formal effects a writer will produce with them cannot, indeed, be predicted from knowing merely these things, but the peculiar quality of the effects when produced will depend in considerable measure on the preconstructional, and often quite unconscious, choices which are thus revealed. That the job of discovering and stating them is not easy will be clear to any one familiar either with the many Marxist attempts to define the position of dead or living authors in relation to the class struggle or with the equally simple-minded efforts of enthusiasts for democracy to find the elements of their creed in (say) Shakespeare and Milton. Here the defect lies primarily in the insensitivity and excessively schematic character of the literary analysis, but the results are frequently vitiated also by the too great readiness of historians who specialize in the social relations of literature to look for the cause of a writer's expression of social attitudes (as Ben Jonson's satiric attacks on usurers, monopolists, speculators, and "undertakers") solely in his personal background and conditioning without allowing for the influence of his poetic ends or the literary tradition he is following or his judgments as to the social prejudices of his audience. The consequence is that first-rate studies of such problems are comparatively rare; I can think of few that seem to me more discriminating and generally sensible than George Orwell's essay on Dickens.

By far the closest relations between literature and society, however, are those which involve the active intervention by writers, as writers, in practical affairs. These are the relations which, on the whole, historians of literature have shown themselves best fitted to deal with; witness, to take only two especially successful examples, the works of Daniel Mornet on the literary preparation for the French Revolution and of Louis Cazamian on the English social novel of the mid-nineteenth century. There have been many such studies, though few as competent or interesting within their limits as these, for most periods of literature—and this means nearly all literary periods—in which the ends that have determined, more or less profoundly, the construction of many literary works are fully explicable only when viewed in a context of the practical and propagandist aims of contemporary politicians, political or ecclesiastical parties, or movements for social revolution or reform. The connections have sometimes been only slight or tangential; at other times— as in the cases of the eighteenth-century French "philosophes" and of that characteristically modern phenomenon, the rise in all countries of a powerful class of Socialist "intellectuals"—they have been extremely close. The literary significance of the productions thus inspired has also varied greatly, from novels and plays which are scarcely more than ephemeral pamphlets with fables, to finished and lastingly moving works of didactic art. The great temptation has been to treat these all alike in terms of the social doctrines or "beliefs" they express without attention to the formal principles which, at least in the better ones, such as Shaw's best plays, have subsumed the practical aims and deflected them from any easily recognizable party line. The historian of forms will attempt a more discriminating analysis, and he will likewise avoid the error of supposing that all novels and plays which have "social significance" in the sense that they are built on contemporary conflicts of the sort that interest sociologists or social historians were therefore necessarily constructed with the depiction of these conflicts as their controlling artistic ends.

105

There remains one important question about causes in literary history to which I can offer here only a somewhat tentative answer. I have tried to make clear in the foregoing discussion that the method of causal investigation appropriate to the history of literary forms is an analytical method presupposing for all literary events a multiplicity of distinguishable causes. The central problem of the historian in this mode is set by his conception of literary works as syntheses of preexistent materials into artistic wholes, the peculiar forms or "powers" of which are determined, within an indefinite range of possible variation among different works, by the specifically different principles of construction their writers have happened to use. His first efforts, therefore, are directed to defining the various forms, in this sense, which have been achieved more or less successfully in the writings he has to deal with. From this as a starting point he proceeds to inquire, first into the extent to which the constitution and handling of the analytically separable elements of object, means, and manner are explicable in the light of the intended forms and the extent to which other reasons must be looked for to account for what was done, and then into the many differentiable antecedent conditions and influences, proximate and remote, without the supposition of which neither the forms aimed at nor the materials of language and human experience in which they are embodied nor the techniques used to construct them would be fully intelligible. This is indeed the only way he can reason if he is to preserve, as completely as possible, the concrete particularity, as artistic objects, of the works that form the events of his history; to reason in the opposite direction would have the effect, as we have seen, of destroying the formal distinctness of the works and of resolving their elements into mere functions of the biographical or social antecedents, whatever these might be, that constitute the historian's preferred causal hypothesis.

It has sometimes been objected to this mode of procedure that it tends to obscure or distort the nature of the facts the historian is studying by directing attention separately to causal factors which in their actual operation are inseparable. And I cannot deny that this is so. It is in one sense false to insist, as critics of the *Scrutiny* school love to do, that such things as plot, character, or thought are merely "abstractions" from the linguistic continuum of a work. For the

106

author they are more than this—they are principles of construction which operate in the process of composition, at times in harmony with one another and at other times in conflict, to determine what he does. Yet, in a different sense, the position of F. R. Leavis and his friends is a perfectly sound one: the immediate response of sensitive readers to a completed work is a response to the synthesis of meaningful words, one after the other, which the writer has effected. And the point becomes clearer still when we turn from the causes in the work which condition its effect on readers to the causes in the author which condition his acts of composition. However these may be differentiated, in relation either to their literary effects or to their personal and collective origins, the manner in which they actually exert their efficacy is again synthetic. The life of an author concentrating on artistic problems in an infinitely complex social and intellectual world, wherein the past is always becoming the present and the present merging into the future, is obviously an indivisible continuity of stimuli and responses. And with respect to these the analytical procedures of the historian of forms, whatever greater understanding they may bring, must always leave one with the sense that much more remains to be said. It is upon these truths that the organic methods of criticism and literary history have been based. But unfortunately, the nature of human language and thinking is such that we cannot have it both ways: either we must sacrifice the organic interconnectedness of things—without denying its reality—for the sake of gaining a sharper understanding of the specific differences among the products of the various literary arts or we must sacrifice these differences—except as they are felt by us apart from what the historian says—for the sake of appreciating the interconnectedness.

There is nothing the historian of forms can do about this objection, therefore, beyond countering it with an equally strong insistence on the limitations of the alternative way of procedure. For his part, he must be content to push his analytical inquiries as far as they can go, and the only question that need perplex him is how far that is. The question arises most acutely when he moves from a consideration of particular lines of development in literature, however complex any of these may be, to a broad view of literary activities that embraces most of the major and many of the minor writings, in all kinds, of several generations or centuries. His first and paramount interest, as a historian of forms, will be to order these in terms of the diversities of ends, materials, and techniques they exhibit and to try to account for them, differentially, in the manner I have suggested. At the same time, however, he cannot help being struck, the farther he goes in his work of comparison, by the extraordinary family resemblances which group together the writings of one generation, no matter how widely different in kind, and separate them as a body more or less sharply from the writings, equally diverse in species, of the generations immediately before and after; a sign of this is his ability to refer anonymous and undated works, with considerable accuracy, to their proper chronological place, without analysis, simply on the strength of the general impressions they make on him. And he will also, as his reading is extended backward and forward in time, come to detect similar strong family resemblances, which likewise cut across distinctions of artistic form, uniting many works of many successive periods and setting them apart as a body from other temporally parallel series of works, in the same language or different languages, the characters of which, though quite distinct, show an equally marked tendency to persist through many generations of writers. From the perception of such resemblances the two complementary ideas of ages and traditions have been derived; and it requires but little reflection to see that they are not, as has sometimes been supposed, merely convenient classificatory fictions but represent real factors in the causation of literary as well as other human activities which no historian of these things is justified in neglecting even though they may not lend themselves readily to analytical investigation.

That there is a peculiar causal force in traditions will scarcely be doubted by any one who has been a member for a decade or more of two universities, or for that matter two well-established institutions of any kind, and has reflected on the different fates which generally befall the same proposals for change, in no matter what aspect of their life, in the one as compared with the other. Each has its own "spirit," hard enough even for those most sensitive to its differentiating effects to formulate and nearly impossible to explain to outsiders, constantly undergoing subtle alteration as new things are done or as new men replace the old yet always exerting, for good or ill, a certain compulsive force on individual and collective choices so that these tend to fall into a general pattern which does not greatly vary, despite external events, from that determined for the institution by its founders. It is the same, as Minto and many others have pointed out, with the churches of the various Protestant denominations. "You might find it hard, if you fixed on details, to say where the difference lies; the same sermon that is preached in one might have been preached in the other; the same hymns might have been sung; yet we feel under the influence of a different spirit. And further, these various churches have probably less in common with each other, though they mix in the same age, than they have with the churches of past ages, each of them perpetuating a traditional spirit of its own, and perhaps making it a point of honour to keep that unchanged." It is the same, too, with philosophy and science; in the long history of these from pre-Socratic Greece to the present, through all the revolutionary shifts in problems, materials, and doctrines, it is possible to trace the persistence, sometimes in clear separation from one another if not in systematic opposition, sometimes in more or less eclectic mixture, of several fundamentally distinct traditions of method, based ultimately perhaps on different temperamental predispositions and different conceptions of the powers of language; the result being that in nearly every period, including our own, we can differentiate among those thinkers who descend from Democritus and the early atomists, those whose master, whether they know it or not, is Plato or Augustine, and those who approach their problems in the spirit of Aristotle. Illustrations could be given from many fields; for our purposes here it will suffice to refer to the three schools of literary history I have distinguished in this essay.

That the same phenomena, finally, present themselves in literature, and probably for similar ultimate reasons, will be granted by every one, although it is harder than in philosophy and science to separate the few great and inclusive traditions from the many secondary ones, deriving from the persistent influence of individual writers (Pindar, Anacreon, Horace, Virgil, Cervantes, and so on), with which literary historians for the most part deal. There are certainly national traditions, however difficult it may be to say wherein any one of them consists; thus, although the novel has become a cosmopolitan genre, we know that we will find some kinds of effects in French novels taken en masse which we do not expect to meet with in English novels and some things in Russian novels that seem exceptional when

109

they occur in novels by either Englishmen or Frenchmen; and so too, perhaps even more strikingly, with poetry and the drama. The existence of these continuities is indeed the great justification of national histories of literature; but there are also, clearly, international literary traditions, the persistence of which can be traced, with occasional interruptions and through multitudinous particular changes in materials, techniques, and forms, from the historical beginnings of artistic writing. The sources of these doubtless lie in basic temperamental differences, such as those which, in nearly all ages and countries, incline some writers to choose the serious and others the comic and satiric forms; some to cultivate "realistic" representations of men as they are or as they are thought to be and others idealized imitations or some mode of "romance"; some to base their art, in a quasi-Aristotelian spirit, on the depiction of human experience in literal terms and others, whether with didactic ends in view or not, on a quasi-Platonic use of analogues and myths. These are persistent causes at once of generic differentiation and generic continuity in literature. Not all of the contrasting effects they make possible are equally prominent in all ages or nations, but once any of these divergent tendencies has asserted itself in the early stages of a given civilization and found distinctive modes of expression, it becomes difficult thereafter, so long as the civilization lasts, for even the most original or revolutionary writers with the same predispositions to make a completely fresh start. The existence of these continuities, impossible though it may be to reduce any of them to satisfactory formulas, is the great justification of "comparative" or "general" histories of literature.

All this could probably have gone without saying; it is much harder to disengage the causal realities which warrant historians in differentiating "periods" or "ages" of literature and in attributing to each of these a distinctive "spirit" or "temper." For one thing, clearly, no solution of continuity can be implied: the processes of change in literature as in all human affairs are obviously unbroken from day to day, year to year, decade to decade, century to century. Nor can we ever be justified in describing "ages" or "periods" in such a way that the radical distinctness of the traditions effective in any of them is concealed. During the past thirty years, for example, I have known well a dozen or more men of some intellectual or literary force, in almost as many different fields, all of whom have seemed to me, as compared with many other equally able older men I have known, to exhibit an essentially "modern" or "twentieth-century" approach to things. Yet their individual backgrounds and interests have been of the most diverse kinds, and could they be brought together in the same room and be set talking with one another about almost any question in which first principles were involved, the result would inevitably be a range of disagreement among them, on philosophy, politics, morality, and art, that would reenact most of the major controversies discoverable in the whole past history of thought. And there is no reason to suppose that this has not always been so—whether for the thirteenth century or the Romantic period—no matter how completely the fact has been concealed—by the synthesizing ambitions of historians.

When we talk about the "spirit" of any age, accordingly, we must be careful to bear these two considerations in mind, but, on the other hand, they need not induce us to give up the problem altogether. For it remains true of my friends as a group that I cannot imagine any other period except our own in which they could have flourished or have developed the particular conceptions and attitudes, fundamentally discordant as these are, which they have held. It is in this sense that they are men of "the new age," even though, from another point of view, only a few of them have been avant-garde revolutionaries and some would certainly be described as conservative traditionalists. When I consider why it is that they have stimulated me more strongly in many ways than most past writers of greater achievement whom I have read, I can only attribute the fact to their common possession of this trait of "modernity." The point has been well put, in negative terms, in the remark of a recent critic that if, for example, "a lost poem of Marvell or a lost motet of Palestrina, each perfect in its kind, were brought forth and presented to a twentieth-century audience as a contemporary work of art, its reception would be dubious. It could at best be applauded as an academic curiosity, a feat of mimicry, or at worst ridiculed as an anachronistic absurdity: it could not be received in the same spirit of serious attention which is accorded a work in some sense felt to be of the moment in which it appears."

Here then is a genuine causal problem, arising for all periods in which literature has flourished and taken on new forms, the solution

111

of which clearly entails giving attention to large collective factors in literary production and appreciation that are not easy to discuss by means of the analytical procedures we have been considering. For what seems to be involved in all such cases of general change is, on the one hand, a more or less rapid increment, in a given generation, of new experiences and interests of all kinds and of new and broadly inclusive ideas for interpreting these and assessing their values relatively to remembered experiences from the past and, on the other hand, the emergence of at least a few writers, intent upon doing fresh things of one sort or another in the various literary arts, who have the ability to invent original forms or to develop old ones in response to the new stimuli. The causes of what we call "modernity" in any age lie in the infinitely complex interaction of these factors as modified by the persistence of many distinct and well-established traditions; and its manifestations, consequently, will always be compatible with the widest diversity in literary species, techniques, and materials.